EARLY IRISH SAINTS

To
Evelyn Gerghty PBVM
(of Glenamaddy and Athenry, Co Galway)
a lady wonderfully gifted with the gentleness of the Lord
this book is dedicated

John J. Ó Ríordáin CSsR

Early Irish Saints

the columba press

First published in 2001 by
the columba press
55A Spruce Avenue, Stillorgan Industrial Park,
Blackrock, Co Dublin

Cover by Bill Bolger
Origination by The Columba Press
Printed in Ireland by ColourBooks Ltd, Dublin
ISBN 1 85607 345 9

Contents

Foreword

According to the once popular song, 'an American landed on Erin's green isle,' and asked 'How can you buy Killarney?' The question raises all sorts of ethical as well as economic and political issues, not least of which is the limitation and, in a certain sense, the poverty of material wealth.

These essays present elements of our Irish heritage that were never for sale, though they were our principal export for centuries and left their mark on the history and culture of Europe. In our present state of material prosperity and cultural change the heritage of the past seems little valued, and yet there are stirrings of renewed interest. Perhaps the youth of today, or tomorrow, will quicken in response to the stories in this book – stories of fine men and women who in their youth felt a generous urge to follow the gospel ideal and unwaveringly pursued it to their dying day. In a wonderful sense they had no interest in the buying or selling of Killarney, but they knew how to enjoy it as a gift of the Creator.

I wrote some of the following chapters while in the Bon Secours Hospital, Glasnevin, Dublin. My room there looked out on the tower of Glasnevin cemetery, not a happy prospect for some perhaps, but for me it was an inspiration because it marked the site of St Mobi's sixth-century monastery where Saints Comgall, Cainnech, Colmcille, Brendan and other saints of whom I was writing had studied and prayed and celebrated their life in Christ. To the present-day saints in the hospital I owe my best thanks – to Catherine O'Loughlin and Sr Mary of the Sacred Heart, and to all the staff. Blessings on them all!

Blessings too on Nuala C. Begley in Dundalk and on Mr Seán

O'Boyle and the staff at Columba Press in Dublin. They and the
Bon Secours saints must have trained in the same school of
Christian excellence and kindly efficency.

I take this opportunity of thanking my friend and confrère
Richard Tobin for checking details of a literary nature. His generosity is such that all I have to do is give him the text and say, in
the words of Eamonn Kelly the *seanchaí*, 'English that for me!'

It was my intention in writing to keep the book simple and
easy to read. Hence the absence of sources, footnotes and the
like. Nevertheless, I wish to acknowledge drawing on such
works as *Vitae Sanctorum Hiberniae* and *Bethada Náem nÉrenn* by
Charles Plummer; *Thesaurus Palaeohibernicus,* edited by Whitley
Stokes and John Strachan; *Lives of the Irish Saints* by John
O'Hanlon; *Patrick in his own words* by Joseph Duffy; *Annals of the
Kingdom of Ireland [Four Masters]* edited by John O'Donovan; *De
Locis Sanctis* by St Adomnán; *The Sources for the Early History of
Ireland* by James F. Kenney; *Irish Monasticism* by John Ryan;
Ireland's Ancient Schools and Scholars by John Healy; *Irish Saints in
Great Britain* by Patrick Moran; *Christianity in Celtic Lands* by
Louis Gougaud; *The Saints of Ireland,* by Mary Ryan D'Arcy; *Irish
Cultural Influence in Europe,* by Tomás Ó Fiaich; *The Catholic
Encyclopaedia; A Calendar of Scottish Saints* by Michael Barrett; *Life
of St Colmcille* by St Adomnán; *Columbanus* by Tomás Ó Fiaich;
Guide to National and Historical Monuments of Ireland by Peter
Harbison; *Two Abbots* by John Silke; *A History of the English
Church and People,* by St Bede; *A Dictionary of Irish Biography* by
Henry Boylan.

May you enjoy reading a little about a small selection from
the vast multitude of saints who have adorned Ireland's early
Christian era and may the wealth of the saints be yours now and
always!

Feast of St Ciarán of Saigher
5 March 2001

Introducing the *Lives* of the Irish Saints

Written *Lives* of Irish saints have survived from mediaeval times. They have come down individually and in collections, in Latin or Irish or both. Individual *Lives* are scattered in manuscripts across Europe; three large collections are to be found in libraries in Brussels, Dublin, and Oxford respectively. Taken collectively the *Lives* form one of the most extensive sources of information relating to the early history of Ireland.

Folkloric Influences

In order to get our twenty-first-century minds attuned to Irish hagiography (that is, the literature treating of the lives and legends of the saints), it is important to have at least some appreciation of the motivation and values which inspired its authors. To take a simple example, 'Rúadán loved cursing' is a phrase occurring in the life of the saint of that name. It is not the kind of thing one expects to find in the life of a saint, but in its context it has a worthy meaning and intentionality.

'Legend belongs to the realm of folklore, where the transmission of facts is exceedingly erratic,' says the scholarly James F. Kenney. 'The folk mind sometimes retains the record of an event with extraordinary accuracy from generation to generation, sometimes within a few years distorts it beyond recognition.' So as Ireland emerged out of paganism and happily and joyfully adapted to Christian ways, it was inevitable that the old mindset did not alter overnight and that certain distortions occurred in the transmission of the Christian story. The *Lives* of early Irish saints reflect this by the inclusion of some thoroughly unChristian legends. So it wasn't that St Rúadán really loved cursing, but as cursing was apparently a druidic practice, Rúadán is presented as up-staging the druids: 'anything you can do I can do better.' In Ireland the phrase 'cursing from a height' still has currency. It was the druidic practice to go up on high ground and issue curses from there so that they might fall with greater force on the object of their malediction. However, there is no question of the early Irish Christian saints being simply 'Christian versions' of old pagan deities, except in the cases of Brigid, Ibar, Ailbe, Senan, and perhaps MacCairthann where some grounds for this belief exist. Nevertheless, as Kenney concludes, 'The Irish saints assuredly are not the successors of Lug and Nuada and Oengus and the Dagda.'

Dates of Composition

The majority of the *Lives* still extant were written from about the tenth to the thirteenth century but they concern saints who had lived in or about the sixth, seventh and eighth centuries; in other words, there is a gap of hundreds years between the life of the saint and his or her *Life*. There are *Lives* of Patrick, Brigid, Colmcille, and Fursa dating from the seventh century but these are exceptions, and though early they are still not contemporary.

Because the *Lives* were written so many centuries after the saints in question had died, they tell us more about the civil and religious climate of the authors' day than that of the subjects'. In the compilation of a *Life* historical facts were difficult to acquire and anyway not considered essential: critical history of our modern kind did not yet exist. But certain literary conventions were followed that gave shape and meaning to the narratives, such as adaptation of material from the Bible, from Egyptian and European monastic traditions, from works by St Jerome and St Gregory the Great, and from a particularly influential *Life* of St Martin of Tours.

The purpose of the Lives

Without doubt the chief purpose in writing the *Lives* of various saints was to honour the person who was regarded as the founder or patron of the church, monastery or local community. This was considered best done by presenting their subject as a 'thaumaturgus', a wonder-worker. Hence, miracle stories and the superhuman practice of virtue were the stock-in-trade of the authors. The compilation of the *Life* was nearly always done at the monastery which guarded the saint's grave or relics. Once done it not only perpetuated the name and fame of the saint but also served as a handbook for pilgrims and a sourcebook for preachers.

A *Life* often helped to explain the relationship between monasteries by inserting legends or facts about the special relationship that existed between their respective founders. In the event of one founder having established several monasteries it helped to explain the composition of the *parouchia* or association of monasteries, for example, the *parouchia* of Colmcille or of St Patrick. These links were important not only in the spiritual domain but frequently involved mundane matters such as rights, dues and privileges. Weight was added to claims and ties by adding layers of legend to show a bond between certain monasteries in olden days or a friendship between the founder of this monastery and that. Then too, the fortune or misfortune of a particular monastery might be explained through the addition of a legend in which the saint was said to have blessed or cursed the place.

Charles Plummer, from whose work together with James F. Kenney's *Sources* I have drawn most of the material for this chapter, notes that in some of the later *Lives*, there is a pronounced venal motive. 'The lowest depths [are] reached perhaps in the life of Caillin in the Book of Fenagh [Co Leitrim], in which eternal damnation is freely awarded as a penalty for being buried in an adjoining parish.'

Sourcing and Salvaging
But how did the names of saints survive all those centuries without having some account of their lives committed to paper? Well, it is a bit like keeping family records. Names of founders of

churches and monasteries were preserved by their local communities in liturgical books such as calendars and martyrologies. These recorded the date of the saint's death so that it would be commemorated and celebrated with each passing year. Besides these, there were various Catalogues and *Féilirí* or Festologies compiled for the same purpose. Notable among these are the *Catalogue of the Saints,* the *Martyrology of Donegal,* the *Féilire of O'Gorman* and the most famous of all, the *Féilire of Oengus.* Some of the documents were in verse form so that they might the more easily be memorised, the *Martyrology of Oengus* being a case in point.

In the years 664-665 the Great Plague swept the country, decimating the monastic population. The same century saw the country bedevilled by the Paschal Controversy which concerned the dating Easter. Taken together they created a break or near break in the continuity of the oral and written tradition. The author of the *Catalogue of the Saints of Ireland* must have been sensitive to the crisis and assembled as much information as possible on the history of the Irish church prior to the plague. Disregarding historical sequence, he gathered all the saints' names at his disposal and divided them into three categories: the most holy, the more holy, and the holy. In broad terms, to category A (432-544) he assigned large number of bishops and founders both native and foreign but all under the leadership of St Patrick. Category B (544-598) included priests for the most part, plus a few bishops; and in Category C (598-665) there are also a few bishops but mostly priests living as hermits. The *Catalogue* probably dates from the eighth century.

The *Martyrology of Oengus* can be more accurately dated to about the year AD 800, and the locus of its composition is Tallaght, Co Dublin. At that time Tallaght under St Maelruain was the vortex of the eighth-century renewal movement known as the *Céilí Dé* reform, and Oengus being a member of the community is popularly styled Oengus the Culdee (from *Céile Dé,* spouse of the Lord). The *Féilire of Oengus* gives a quatrain for each day of the year in which the name and a brief comment is given on the saint or saints to be commemorated.

The *Martyrology of O'Gorman* is of twelfth-century date and the work of Máel-Maire Ua Gormáin, abbot of the monastery of Knock, a little to the east of Louth village, who died in 1181. Abbot O'Gorman specifically states that his purpose in writing is to expand the list of saints mentioned by Oengus and to correct errors in his assignment of feast days. He further wished to give more prominence to saints on the universal calendar – a sign of the times, because the twelfth-century reform was well under way by then. O'Gorman's *Féilire* commemorates no less than 3,450 saints from biblical and general hagiographical sources.

Further lists of saints are to be found in the *Martyrology of Donegal*, in Cuimmín's *Poem on the Saints of Ireland*, in the *Tallaght (Stowe) Missal*, and in *The Breviary of Aberdeen*. This latter is chiefly the work of Bishop Elphinstone (1483-1514) who also found time to build the beautiful cathedral of Old Aberdeen.

A Salute to the Masters
The centuries from the sixteenth to the nineteenth were thoroughly troubled times both religiously and politically in Ireland. The persecution carried on by the English-Protestant ruling class not only involved the suppression of the monasteries and the sequestering to the Crown of England of all property owned by the Catholic Church, but also an iconoclastic campaign which brought about the destruction of untold numbers of ancient manuscripts and works of art. Fr John Colgan (1592-1658) from near Carndonagh, Co Donegal, together with some of his Franciscan confrères, notably Aodh Mac an Bháird (Hugh Ward) and Patrick Flemming, committed himself to collecting and publishing surviving manuscript material relating to Irish church history and lives of Irish saints. To forward this project, Ward sent Brother Michael O'Cleary to Ireland in 1626 to copy any appropriate material that had survived. This ultimately resulted in the compilation of *The Annals of Ireland*, better known as *The Annals of the Four Masters* – a term coined by Colgan. Colgan himself published the first volume of the *Acta Sanctorum*, or *Lives of the Saints*, in Louvain 1645. It was followed in 1647 by

Triadis Thaumaturgae Acta, or *Lives of the Three Wonder-workers,*
containing *Lives* of Patrick, Brigid and Colmcille; and eight years
later, by a work on John Duns Scotus, whom Colgan claimed to
be Irish. It was Colgan's hope to publish seven or eight volumes
but ill health, lack of financial resources, and ultimately death
overtook him with less than half his ambition fulfilled.

There is much work still to be done.

A guide to some of the place-names mentioned in this book

St Patrick

There's an old Irish ballad which runs,

St Patrick was a gentleman; he came of decent people;
He built a church in Dublin town, and on it put a steeple.

That the saint was a gentleman can hardly be doubted. We can also assume that his family were probably a decent enough lot even though their faith seems to have been slack. After that, the balladeer takes off into a world of fantasy and folk tradition.

Perhaps the most famous representation of St Patrick of Ireland is an engraving made in 1642 by Fr Thomas Messingham. Versions of it dating from the early twentieth century present Patrick as tall and venerable, robed in green vestments, holding up a shamrock as a catechetical aid before King Laoghaire or pointing down to the water at his expulsion of the snakes. When the historians got to work on this image they showed that the story about the shamrock dates only from the seventeenth century and the one about the snakes probably dates from Viking times, around the year 1,000.

Although these legends are not historically factual, they are not to be dismissed as empty and untrue. They do express truths about St Patrick: the Trinity was central to his life and teaching; and while he may not have encountered snakes in Ireland such as the ones you see in the zoo, he did expel the evil that is symbolised by the snake.

Facts of history

But what historical facts do we know? Well, we know that St Patrick existed and roughly when – namely, the fifth century AD. We know 'that he was a bishop in Ireland; that he came from

15

Britain where his father had been of the Roman official class and
well-to-do.' We know that he devoted much of his life to
evangelising the Irish people, baptising them in large numbers.
However, the most real and rounded Patrick emerges from the
pages of his own writings. Two of these survive, the *Confession*
and the *Letter to Coroticus*. Together they make up about thirty
pages of a modern book. But they are full of information, mainly
about 'his character, his faith, his vision,his understanding of
God'. From the two documents it is evident that we are dealing
with an able and well-informed man. There are, for example, 72
books in the Bible; Patrick, in his few short pages makes reference or alludes to 54 of them. He also refers to twenty of those
early Christian scholars, theologians and saints whom we know
collectively as the Fathers of the Church; and finally, he makes
reference to eight church councils. In other words, he is familiar
with almost every major meeting of bishops and scholars down
to his own time.

Contrary to popular opinion, we are not dealing here with a
poor uneducated man. Those who have imagined him to be a
simple-minded, inarticulate, incoherent sort of person need to
think again. His life is enveloped in the consciousness of being
under orders from Christ to bring the gospel to the Irish. This is
the basis of his unflinching steadfastness and confidence as he
faces criticism of his mission. His genius often comes across, not
directly in what he says, but in what he means – a characteristic
readily understood in Ireland.

Patrick's exact place of origin continues to baffle scholars.
England, Scotland, Wales, and Boulogne-sur-mer in France,
have all been mentioned. He was born into a Christian home,
and presumably got a good grounding in the faith. But in his
own honest way he admits that in his teens he and his companions didn't pay any great attention to the advice of the priests,
and in later years he regretted this.

The first serious crisis in his life occurred when he was kid-
napped and sold into slavery in Ireland. He was sixteen at the
time, and if ever a youngster got a rude awakening, it was he.

From his writing, one can glean that his family were, materially speaking, fairly comfortable. Now in exile, he was anything but, as he found himself alone in a herdsman's shed or under the open canopy of heaven. Curiously enough, it was in these surroundings of isolation that he matured in his faith. With all the time in the world to think, and the silence and the darkness of the night around him, he came to realise that in all the upheaval there was one constant element: God. And there in an Irish countryside the homesick teenager fell on his knees to pray – real prayer, a pouring out the contents of his troubled soul to the Lord. At sixteen Patrick had grown up. Boredom had vanished. There was determination and direction in his life and God was at the heart of it. Many years later, in his *Confession*, he wrote: 'My faith grew stronger and my zeal so intense that in the course of a single day I would say as many as a hundred prayers and almost as many in the night. This I did even when I was in the woods and on the mountains. Even in times of snow or frost or rain I would rise before dawn to pray. I never felt the worse for it; nor was I in any way lazy because, as I now realise, I was full of enthusiasm.' That enthusiasm was to be a hallmark of Patrick's entire life.

After six years in slavery, Patrick made a successful bid to escape. He walked about two hundred miles across Ireland until he found a trading ship bound for the continent. After some initial disappointment, he was taken on board, and after three days at sea landed in the west of France. For a further twenty eight days the party journeyed on through desolate lands, encountering nobody and enduring hunger and hardship. He finally made his way to his relatives in Britain but not before enduring a further two months of captivity.

Now that he was home, his relatives wished him to stay, but Patrick, in a dream, heard 'The voice of the Irish' calling him to return and walk among them once more. With that generosity of heart characteristic of the man, he studied for the priesthood, was later ordained bishop, and sent on a mission to Ireland. For this he was well fitted, for besides his religious formation, he had from his slavery days, a knowledge of the language and customs of the Irish together with long experience of the climatic conditions of this north Atlantic island.

His missionary career was spectacular. True, he wasn't the very first to bring the Christian message to Ireland, but his coming was highly significant. Without brag or boast he sets out the facts of what happened. He tells us that he 'baptised thousands', 'ordained clerics everywhere', 'gave presents to kings', 'was put in irons', 'lived in daily expectation of murder, treachery or captivity', 'journeyed everywhere in many dangers, even to the farthest regions beyond which no man dwells', and rejoiced to see 'the flock of the Lord in Ireland growing splendidly with the greatest care and the sons and daughters of kings becoming monks and virgins for Christ.'

His life in Christ
Patrick came to love God because he realised more and more how God loved him first. The very thought of what God had done for him moved him to spontaneous prayer. He had a deep sense of the Holy Spirit of God living within him, praying within him, supporting, guiding, and guarding him. He tells us, for example, that it was the Spirit who persuaded him not to leave Ireland when he felt like a visit to Britain and France. And it was the Spirit who 'called out on his behalf' in a particularly severe bout of depression. The Holy Trinity whom he loved and adored inspired all his labours. He was unconcerned about personal material gain or physical security.

Referring to his *Confession* and *Letter to Coroticus*, Fr Daniel Conneely (on whose work I am drawing liberally in this essay) says that Patrick 'shows a real sense of the presence of Christ and of God's providence in his life. He has absolute trust in God's loving care for him. He is full of love for God; full of joy and pride in his missionary vocation and of gratitude to God for the gift of it. So great is his prayerfulness and feeling for prayer that talking to God and of God are as natural to him as breathing in the air, or absorbing the warmth and light of the sun.'

He sees 'everything in his life as a gift from God, both in its small beginnings and in its growth, and perseverance too is to be prayed for. In his latter years – the years of the *Confession* and *Letter* – looking back on a life crowded with bodily and spiritual trials, and crowded equally with great joys, he has come to see the pattern: the golden thread of God's loving providence woven into it all.'

Like St Paul and St Augustine, Patrick sees himself as worthless, but with the grace of God assisting him, he is ready for anything. His mission to Ireland is seen by him as an astounding gift of God. The mission was God's idea, not his own. God had promised to bring salvation to the ends of the earth, and here was Patrick at the very edge of the known world, gathering in the Irish for Christ. For this he gives unwearying thanks to God and prays unceasingly for the grace to be faithful to the end.

His relevance today
'Many inspirational benefits are associated with St Patrick's pastoral letters,' says Fr Conneely, 'but their crucial relevance today lies:

(i) in their communication of faith as life with Christ;

(ii) in their proclamation of the *absolute value to Christ* of every single human being everywhere; and

(iii) in the way in which, while being supremely active and practical, St Patrick always kept in sight, like an horizon, that his pastoral objective was transforming minds and hearts .'

'In these three aspects,' he says, 'the Western world has become seriously flawed as a witness to Christian life.' It has knowledge of Christianity but doesn't have much sense of Christ in our midst. It has a kind of technical knowledge of Jesus, rather than a personal relationship with him. For St Patrick, his Catholic faith wasn't simply belief in a number of truths. It was that, and he lists them, but it was an utterly trusting relationship with Christ Jesus and with the Holy Trinity. Everything was their gift to him – his conversion, his vocation, his successful mission to the Irish. Every dark cloud coming down upon him, every ray of sunshine

illuminating his life, was all interpreted in the light of the grace
of God at work in him and around him, a God who held the
whole world in his hands and who loved Patrick personally.

Kyrie Eleison and Deo Gratias
One of our most ancient manuscripts, the *Book of Armagh,* tells us
that Patrick wished the Irish to have two phrases ever on their
lips, *Kyrie Eleison* and *Deo Gratias;* Lord have mercy, and Thanks
be to God. It was between those two prayers that Patrick lived
out his own full and saintly life. It is where we, too, will find the
fulness of life – trusting in the forgiveness of the One who loves
us, and eternally grateful for everything.

St Brigid

St Brigid, whose name means 'the exalted one', is Patroness of Ireland. What we know about her life, historically, is minimal. And yet, most people will have images of her, drawn perhaps from childhood memories, customs and devotions associated with her feast, or personal experience of her assistance. Brigid is venerated not only in Ireland and Britain but also across the continent in France, Germany, Switzerland, Italy and elsewhere. In Germany she was invoked as the patron and protectress of travellers and pilgrims. Mediaeval knights adopted her as their patron; and it was these gentlemen in shining armour who began the custom of calling the girls they married their *brides* – a variant of the name Brigid. And even today, it is to Brigid that many women look for inspiration in their search for models, prototypes, and symbols of the feminine in human life.

Treating of Brigid, Dr Dáithí Ó hÓgáin writes 'The earliest surviving reference to her dates from around the year 600. It occurs in an origin story of the Fotharta Sept, and in it she is stated to have been of that Sept and is called "truly pious 'Brig-eoit" and described as "another Mary" ... At the request of the Kildare church a Latin biography of the saint, *Vita Brigitae,* was compiled in or about the year 650 by a cleric known as Cogitosus. A striking feature of this work is the lack of real information on the historical Brigid, who had lived in the previous century.'

Brigid, a Bridge
In the absence of any detailed historical data on Brigid, we may well ask why she enjoys such prominence. She is among the first fruits of Irish Christianity. Her life (c. AD 455-525) spans the

years between St Patrick's mission and the spectacular rise of
monasticism in the sixth century. Furthermore, Brigid was not
only a holy woman, but the foundress of what is probably the
earliest known monastery in Ireland, Kildare. Although the
monastic movement in the church of the fifth century was vib-
rant on the continent, there is no Irish monastery going back to
that century with the possible exception of Kildare.

Brigid, a Princess
Brigid's father, Dubthach (Duffy), is described as being of the
nobility, while her mother, Broicsech (Brocessa), was a slave,
and only a subordinate wife. The father is thought to have been
a pagan and the mother a Christian. It is said that because of the
jealousy of Dubthach's primary wife, Brocessa was banished to
Fochard-Muirthemhne in the Dundalk area, before the birth of
Brigid. Modern research would seem to favour the territory of
Fotharta Airbrech near Croghan Hill on the Offaly-Kildare border as the birthplace of the saint.

Brigid, a Bishop!
Brigid is said to have been fostered out to a woman who saw to
her education in literary pursuits, practical domesticity, and
farm management. She is also said to have turned down some
good offers of marriage, a fact which enraged her father. But
Brigid was from first to last a mettlesome lady, and having
dedicated her virginity to the Lord, she was not going to be de-
flected from her purpose. Traditions vary as to the location and
circumstances of her religious profession. Broccán's Hymn says
that herself and seven other young women went to Cruachan Bri
Ele in Offaly 'to have the order of penance' conferred on them by
Bishop Mel. The bishop was happy to oblige them, but in error
'Bishop Mel conferred on Brigid the episcopal order.' Asked afterwards why he had read the wrong prayers, Mel replied that
the Holy Spirit had taken the matter out of his hands! Ever afterwards Brigid's successors enjoyed the privileges of a bishop.
    There was one virtue in Brigid which outshone all others and

to which the *Lives* incessantly refer. It was her liberal hand. The poor of Christ she could never refuse. From childhood to death the story is the same. Food, clothing, livestock, her father's jewelled sword, the bishop's precious vestments, the nuns' festive dinner, all went the same road – to the poor. Her resourcefulness and improvisation in alleviating the circumstances of the needy are legendary and she is often presented as having food multiply in her generous hands. When it came to serving the poor, nothing was sacrosanct; nothing but the requirements of the poor themselves. 'If I had the power,' she is quoted as saying, 'to give away the whole Kingdom of Leinster, I would willingly give it to God' (i.e. God's poor).

Brigid, a Mystic

What distinguishes the Brigidine style of spirituality from all others, according to author Alice Curtayne, is 'its charming pastoral character'. A *Life* of Brigid in the *Leabhar Breac* presents the nun of Kildare meeting St Brendan the Navigator: 'She came from her sheep to welcome Brendan.' Crossing a ploughed field she and Brendan exchanged spiritual thoughts. Brendan owned that he never stepped over seven furrows without turning his mind and heart to God, but Brigid confided to him that since the first day she set her mind on the Lord, the thought of him had never been out of her head. And Broccán's Hymn from the late sixth or early seventh century gives us a glimpse of what these thoughts might be:

Deeper than the seas,
Greater than words can express,
Three Persons in One only God;
Overflowing with wonder.

Brigid, a Model

The Brigidine story, coming as it did at the dawn of Irish Christianity, presented Ireland with an entirely new model of womanhood and the Irish loved her for it. In daring and innovative ways she is presented as expressing the gospel injunction of loving God and neighbour. She is described as travelling the land – traditionally in her two-horse chariot – spreading the good news of Jesus, healing the sick, tempering the mighty and raising the lowly, and tending her sheep on 'Brigid's Pasture,' that 5,000 acre plane otherwise known as the Curragh of Kildare. Even the rich Celtic imagination was at a loss to describe such a lover of Christ. And then it came: she was the nearest thing to the Mother of God; she was the Mary of the Gael, Mary of the Irish.

Her death

According to tradition, some time in the middle of the 520s AD, on 1 February the great lady received the last rites of the church at her monastery in Kildare and it was there she died, and in the monastic church was laid to rest. Her tomb, on the right hand side of the altar, was held in the greatest veneration for centuries, but it is claimed that because of the Viking terror, her body was translated about AD 835 or earlier to Downpatrick Cathedral and placed in one tomb with the relics of Patrick, and later those of Colmcille. On 9 June 1186, shortly after the Norman invasion, the relics of all three saints were moved again. This latter move was at the instigation of John de Coursey, the Norman conqueror of Down, and may have been inspired by a political motive to ingratiate the the new overlords with their Irish subjects.

Her legacy

Whether or not Brigid inherited various attributes associated with a pagan goddess of the same name, whether she was born in Offaly, Kildare or Louth, and whether she died on 1 February, are not important in the long run. The foundress of Kildare is enshrined in tradition as a woman who walked with God, totally dedicated to Christ his Son, loving him, living for him, and in turn being sustained by his love. This is the deepest truth about this wonderful woman – deeper than mere historical facts can convey. As with St Patrick, as with all saints, saints are people who live and move and have their being in Jesus, recognising him as their Lord and Saviour, seeing life through his eyes, making decisions big and small in the light of his gospel.

In the ancient Irish calendar, 1 February was one of the four hinges on which the year swung, the others being 1 May, 1 August and 1 November. Each had its own specific festival, namely, *Imbolg, Bealtaine, Lúnasa* and *Samhain* respectively. It would seem that pre-Christian Ireland celebrated a pagan goddess, Brigit by name, who is thought to have been associated with agricultural fertility and was seen as a guardian goddess of domestic animals. It is possible that in the new Christian Ireland, our St Brigid, sharing the same name as the goddess, had all the associations with fertility and farming transferred to her. As G. K. Chesterton wrote in his book on St Francis of Assisi, 'Pagans were wiser than paganism; that is why they became Christians.'

Setting St Brigid's Feast at *Imbolg,* then, is significant. By 1 February, the worst of the winter is considered to be over. There is change in the degree of light and dark that surrounds, things are beginning to sprout and grow, young men's fancies are turning to thoughts of love. This is a time of propagation or impending propagation. Fisher folk are checking their nets and boats; farmers are preparing to till the soil and put in crops; the animals, both domestic and wild, are giving birth to their young. (In fact the term *Imbolg* means 'giving birth to'.) The festival of *Imbolg,* then, is a real turning point. The commemoration of the Nun of Kildare on this date is a statement that St Brigid, the woman of abundance, is ushering in a new dawn, an era of light, and life and hope, for a new and Christian Ireland.

We leave the final word to the late Alice Curtayne, who herself wrote an inspiring life of the saint:

Nine hundred years were to elapse before anything resembling the Brigidine group was to appear on the continent of Europe, when at length its counterpart was seen in the *cenacolo* of Catherine Benincasa, later called St Catherine of Sienna, whose 'family' preceded all the famous 'salons' of Europe. It was one hundred years after that before a woman, in the person of the divine poetess, Vittoria Colonna, proved again that she could be at once leader and inspiration of an intellectual re-birth. In France there was nothing remotely resembling such feminine initiative until the seventeenth century; and in England nothing that in the least recalled it until the nineteenth century ... very astonishing indeed is the discovery that the feminine inspiration which delighted Europe in later centuries down to modern times was already an accepted feature of the early Irish church.'

St Colmcille

Saints seem to be people of many parts and Colmcille more than most: he was a prince, priest, prophet, poet, diplomat, monk, abbot, scribe, and scholar. In terms of family background, he sprung from the Cenél Conaill (the O'Donnells of Donegal), a branch of the royal house of the Clan Uí Néill. He was a descendant of Niall of the Nine Hostages, and over a period of 700 years, his family produced as many as forty-one High Kings. Colmcille, too, it seems, was himself eligible for such an office.

By secular as well as by religious standards he is one of the outstanding figures of Early Mediaeval Ireland. Speculation about his life, his reasons for leaving Ireland, or the extent of his influence at home and abroad, cannot detract from that fact. Nor can a case be made against his holiness on the grounds that he was not formally canonised by the Pope, because Colmcille lived hundreds of years prior to such formalities. When St Adomnán wrote his *Life* in the seventh century, it was specifically to establish for all and sundry that the first abbot of Iona was a man who walked with God in a truly extraordinary and inspiring fashion. For fourteen hundred years the Christian community, particularly in Ireland and Scotland, has acknowledged this estimation of the man by invoking his intercession and keeping his memory green.

From the various sources at our disposal it is possible to put reasonable shape on his life while bearing in mind that the only fairly certain date in his career is at the end. On the testimony of St Adomnán, his biographer, the saint died on Iona on 9 June, AD 597, aged 75. At the other end of the scale, the traditional date of his birth is 7 December, AD 521, and the place is Gartan, Co Donegal.

His training

In his childhood, Colmcille was fostered by a local priest named Cruithnechán, who not only taught the boy his letters and his prayers but gave him a shining personal example of Christian living, so shining indeed, that he too, like his young foster-child, is venerated as a saint of God. It was during these years of fosterage that his peers, observing the boy's frequent visits to the little chapel, dubbed him Colm Cille, dove of the church, an affectionate title which has attended him ever since in Ireland, while the Scots have a preference for the Latin, Columba, a dove.

When his term of fosterage was completed Colmcille, instead of following the way of a prince among his people, opted to become a Christian monk. Such a choice on the part of so highborn a young man had major consequences for the young and evolving Irish church. His career undoubtedly provided a powerful stimulus to monastic development, and his choice of the monastic life was a headline followed by many another young nobleman. He was a man of the very highest birth, with all the natural advantages which such a circumstance gave in an aristocratic society. He had the gift of second sight, combined with a power to control others by the sheer force of his own personality. He was a shrewd judge of character, and yet a man of warm sympathies. His magnetism not only influenced the monks and the laity; even the animals felt his attraction. He could command, he could comfort, he could delight. A recruit with such qualities must have outshone most of his contemporaries.

The traditions handed down indicate that, having departed from his saintly foster-father, he studied under St Finnian of Moville, St Enda of Aran, Gemman the Bard, and St Finnian of Clonard, 'the teacher of the saints of Ireland'. It is said that he received the diaconate from St Finnian of Moville, and that he was ordained to the priesthood by St Etchin at the monastery of Clonfad, near Kinnegad. At the time of ordination Colmcille is estimated to have been about thirty years of age.

According to St Aengus of Tallaght, he next set out for St Mobi's monastery at Glasnevin in the company of three friends

– Comgall of Bangor, Ciaran of Clonmacnoise and Canice of Kilkenny. Their stay was short-lived because Mobí disbanded the community at the onset of the *Buidhe Chonnaill* or Yellow Plague. Colmcille, it is said, returned to his native territory, and established a monastery in Derry, a city which ever since proudly bears his name, *Doire Cholm Cille,* Derry of Colmcille.

His Foundations

Information on Colmcille's life prior to his departure for Britain in AD 563, is little enough. During the decade prior to his departure he was active in establishing monastic communities throughout the upper half of Ireland where his family held sway. Among these foundations were Swords, Lambay, Tory, Drumcliffe, Drumcolumb, Clonmore, Moone, Inchmore in Lough Gowna, and perhaps Kells. There is no knowing the full number, but St Dallan Forgaill, in his *Amra* or Elegy of Colmcille, describes him as 'guardian of a hundred churches'; and not to be outdone, the compiler of *The Martyrology of Donegal,* declares:

Three hundred he measured, without fault,
Of churches fair, 'tis true;
And three hundred, lasting books
Noble-bright he wrote.

Of all his foundations, Iona in Scotland and Durrow in Co Laois are the best authenticated.

His missionary exile

In his youth he had renounced the family inheritance. Then, at the age of 42, he was prepared to go a step further and renounce his native land. In Early Christian Ireland, the greatest sacrifice and penance a monk could undertake, other than martyrdom, was voluntary exile. Colmcille, who wasn't in the habit of doing things by halves, took that penitential option. The world of folk-lore has made much play out of Colmcille secretly making a copy of a Psalm book belonging to St Finnian of Moville, of his alleged involvement – even by prayer – in the Battle of Cúl

Dreimne, and his subsequent excommunication – wrongfully as it happens – at the Synod of Tailtiu and a penance imposed by St Molaise about going into exile for life. Adomnán simply states that he left Ireland 'because he wished to become a pilgrim for Christ's sake,' and St Bede, the English historian, confirming this, says that 'there came from Ireland into Britain, a famous priest and abbot, a monk by habit and life, whose name was Columba, to preach the Word of God.' His going must have been a source of sorrow to many for he was not only holy, but an admirable and attractive man in so many ways – tall, handsome and affable, a poet of high accomplishment, a man born to rule, with a sweetness and power in his voice said to have been verging on the miraculous.

To this day the people of Islay maintain that when the saint sailed out from Derry he made first landfall on their island, but then moved on to another Inner Hebridean Island, Iona, for his first permanent settlement in Scotland. Here, for thirty four years he would lead his monks in prayer, study and apostolic endeavour. Life was rarely less than grim on that island, and yet, it was here that he founded a scribal tradition which ultimately produced the Book of Kells; and it was from here that he guided and conducted a mission to both his own Gaelic people in the kingdom of Scottish Dal Riada and to the pagan Pictish peoples further north. Nobody knows for sure the extent of this work. What we do know is that the history and topography of Scotland and its islands would never be the same because of the journeying and missionary activities of these soldiers of Christ.

During the Iona years Colmcille returned to Ireland on several occasions, and for various reasons. The monastery of Durrow, in Co Laois, was almost certainly founded during one of these visits, while on another, at the celebrated Convention of the Kings, at Drumcet near Limavady, he negotiated the independence of Scottish Dal Riada and saved the bards from suppression. He visited or maintained contact with other Irish church leaders, and many of them in turn visited Iona. Adomnán's *Life* offers a vision of a community of saints and founders bound together in strong brotherly relations.

Many of Adomnán's stories testify to the gentleness of the founding Abbot of Iona, be it the rehabilitation of a robber, or the counselling of a distraught woman in a bad marriage, or the offering of shelter and protection to a tired crane that had flown in from Ireland, or in coping with the emotional upset of the old white horse that sensed his master's death approaching. So involved was he in the everyday life of the community that, even in the remoteness of Iona, he still felt the need to find a quiet place for prayer in a hermitage by the western ocean.

On occasion he worked miracles, but never where simple good sense would suffice. Thus, he warned one of the brethren not to presume on God's providence by taking short cuts across the open sea to Tiree but to take the safer route by island-hopping. His relationship with nature was practical and respectful.

By the end of his life, Colmcille's achievement was monumental: he had founded Iona and a number of connected monasteries in the west of Britain and in Ireland, and had exercised strong and decisive influence over the political scene in Scotland and Ireland. But he would have considered these achievements minor in comparison to what he was seeking to attain, namely, wisdom, learning and holiness. Judging from the *Amra Colmcille*, by the time of his death the saint already had an incomparable reputation for these virtues, the virtues not just of a saint but of a wholly rounded and complete human being.

St Enda

Although direct historical knowledge of Enda the man is sketchy, there is abundant testimony to his extraordinary formative influence on many of the key figures and movements in the Irish church of his time. Like Brigid, he is in the nature of a 'bridging figure'. His adult life spanned the last decades of the fifth century and perhaps three decades of the next. Since he was of royal stock, his choice of the monastic life must have been a highly influential one. He is said to have been the son and heir of Conall, King of Oriel, whose dominions roughly corresponded to the combined counties of Louth, Monaghan, Armagh, and Fermanagh.

Christian tradition assigns Enda four sisters, one of whom, Fanchea, a nun, had a strong influence on his conversion to faith in Christ Jesus, and later encouraged him to adopt the monastic life. It would appear that shortly after becoming a Christian he renounced his royal status, disposed of his assets, which were very considerable, and began to live the monastic or heremitical life at Killany, between Dundalk, Co Louth and Carrickmacross, Co Monaghan.

Because Irish Christianity was only in its infancy at the time, Enda had few, if any, role models in Ireland. He therefore crossed the North Channel to St Martin's Monastery in Galloway, which at that time enjoyed a high reputation for scripture study and general training in the discipline of monastic life. That monastery, founded by St Ninian in or about AD 397, is known as *Rosnat* in later Irish tradition, and in the Latin as the *Magnum Monasterium*, the Great Monastery (because of its reputation), or *Candida Casa*, the White House (because of the light shade of the stonework of the church). In going to *Rosnat,* Enda would seem to have been a trend setter, because countless young men of later days would follow on his footsteps, among them Tighernach of Clones, Eoghan of Ard Straw, Coirpre of Coleraine, and Finnian of Moville.

After some time at *Rosnat,* Enda returned to Ireland via the Boyne estuary at Drogheda. Here at the southern end of his erstwhile dominions the newly trained monk and ordained priest devoted himself to church building, both spiritual and physical, on both sides of that historic river. Despite the good work done by him in this part of the country, Enda's name and reputation was for ever to be linked with the west. His status as 'father of Irish monasticism' was earned on the Aran Islands, where in a spot still bearing his name, he established Ireland's first great monastery for men. Pre-Christian Aran had been dominated by one name, that of Aengus associated with the spectacular *Dún,* or fort. Christian Aran is also dominated by a single name, Enda, embodied in the village of Killeany, which Enda chose as the place of his burial, 'the place of his resurrection'.

Mediaeval folklore does not confine Enda's arrival in Aran to a mere boat trip, not a conventional boat at any rate. There is a large stone on the shore beside the monastic settlement known in tradition as 'the curragh stone' or *Bád na Naomh* (the saint's boat). The accompanying legend attests that this is the very craft on which Enda came sailing over the waves. And the legend would also have us know that Corban, the local pagan chief, was completely bewildered by the sight, and took to his heels across the sea to north Clare. Having lost both his head and his island in most ungallant circumstances, he felt truly deflated. From the safety of Corcomroe he decided to conduct a controlled experiment before taking any further action. To this end he filled a cask with corn and took it down to the shore. Here he made a pact with himself declaring the if St Enda was of God the cask would make its own way to him in Aran without human help. With that, the legend concludes, the cask was wafted over the waves to Enda at the little harbour which ever since bears the name *Port Daibhche,* the Harbour of the Cask.

'Aran of the Saints', Ara na Naomh

Enda's reputation as a giant of singular holiness and austerity spread among young idealistic men of his time to such a degree that mediaeval authors, setting out to write the life of any other Irish holy man, felt compelled to state that at some time or other he had done a stint in Aran. This association with Enda put the reputation of the new man beyond question. Accordingly, we are presented with a plethora of saints said to have trained in Enda's establishment; a worthy notion indeed, but confusing for the historian. Here, according to the saints' *Lives*, came the men who by their own reputations and foundations were to change the face of Ireland forever: St Finnian of Cloanard (d. 549), St Ciarán of Clonmacnoise (d. 545 or 549), St Colmcille of Derry and Iona (d. 597), St Brendan the Navigator (d. 570s?), St Jarlath of Tuam (d. 550s?), St Finian of Moville (d. 570s?), St Kevin of Glendalough (d. 618), and a host of others. So many attained outstanding holiness in Aran under Enda and the abiding influence of his spirit, that the islands were acclaimed 'the novitiate of the Irish saints' or more affectionately *Ara na Naomh*, Aran of the Saints.

There are numerous ancient churches, oratories, cells and other relics of the Christian era scattered across the islands. Church dedications are liberal: to Kevin, Gobnait, Ciarán, The Seven Princes, The Four Beauties, The Canons – now demolished – and, possibly, The Vigils. The two most extensive and impressive monastic sites, however, are at opposite ends of Inishmore, namely, Killeany to the east and The Seven Churches to the west.

At the The Seven Churches (*Na Seacht dTeampaill*) is the grave of St Brecin, the founder, together with a church dedicated to his memory, and other buildings. St Enda's foundation towards the other end of the island is marked by a little church bearing his name, *Teighleach Éanna*. On the hill above stands *Teampall Benain*, St Benan's Church, said to be the tiniest in Europe.

While Benan himself may never have set foot on Aran, the captivating little church pitched high on the hill against the sky-line is a constant reminder of this charming man with a beautiful voice who became first successor to St Patrick in the See of Armagh. Of his early missionary life it is related that a young Leinster princess fell madly in love with him, not only because of his general manliness and grace, but in sheer rapture at hearing him singing the psalms and teaching the melodies to the people. Like many a teenage girl in like circumstances, she lived to get over it, but according to the story, it took a dash of holy water blessed by St Patrick himself to bring her back from death's door. From then on, we are told, she continued to love Benan but with a mature and profound affection.

Two great favourites in Irish hagiographical lore are Ciarán of Clonmacnoise and Colmcille of Derry and Iona. Their time in Aran at St Enda's monastery is remembered in many ways both in written and oral sources, as well as in placenames such as *Mainistir Chiaráin* (Ciarán's Monastery) and *Tobar Cholmcille* (St Colmcille's Well). Ciarán was the best loved of all the monks in Aran, for he was a fine, generous-hearted and deeply spiritual man. Among his labours in the autumn, we are told, was the harvesting of the corn crop – a thought to keep in mind when strolling or biking through *Fearann an Choirce* (Oatquarter). The angels are said to have given considerable help to Ciarán in his task of grinding the corn in the querns, though Colmcille is said to have played his part as well.

Holy Rivalry
One might say that neither Ciarán nor Colmcille were overburdened with work as far as reaping and milling were concerned because the islands are spare in arable land. The shortage of land for cultivation is probably at the root of a charming little legend which tells of how the boundary between the two principal monastic foundations on the island was rather unevenly established. The two abbots, Enda and Brecin, agreed to divide the island between them on the basis that each should begin to celebrate Mass in his own monastery at dawn, and having done so, proceed to walk in the direction of the other. Their meeting point would become the boundary.

Well, it so happened that St Brecin, being a little too enthusiastic for the welfare of his community, started Mass ahead of the
agreed time and thereby gained a walking advantage over Enda.
The latter, however, in the depth of his prayerfulness detected
the cheating and invoked God on his side, with the result that
Brecin and his contingent were stopped in their tracks. Stuck to
the ground they were, there by the sea at Kilmurvey, and
couldn't move an inch until Enda arrived. The boundary was
established at that spot, and remained so ever after.

Here in Aran the monks prayed, here they observed rigorous
fasts and long vigils, because Enda more than all others was
renowned for the severity of his rule. Rigorous though he was in
matters of personal and community discipline, there was always
a warm humanity to temper austerity. The mediaeval *Lives* recount that when St Brendan the Navigator visited Aran to con-
sult Enda on his proposed voyage of exploration, the meagre
monastic fare was abandoned in favour of spring lamb and
wholemeal bread, because in Aran, as elsewhere in Christian
Ireland, the guest is always Christ.

A thousand years after the death of Enda, the Archbishop of
Tuam made an impressive inventory of the churches and holy
places of Aran. In his time and for long after, Enda's grave was
still pointed out; and not only Enda's but the graves of one hundred and twenty seven other saints as well, not to mention the
multitude whose holiness is known only to God. Tread softly,
then, on *Ara na Naomh;* 'take off your shoes, for the place on
which you stand is holy ground.'

St Brendan the Navigator

St Brendan is known the world over as the man at the centre of the *Navigatio Sancti Brendani* (The Voyage of St Brendan), the medieval saga about his voyage to what is today known as North America. In the dioceses of Kerry and Clonfert,Co Galway, however, he is revered as a great monastic founder and invoked as diocesan patron.

Prior to the 1970s when Tim Severin and his companions made a successful crossing of the North Atlantic in an early mediaeval-style craft, the *Navigatio* was often dismissed as a highly fanciful tale. Now, however, it belongs to the realm of serious historical debate. Tim Severin has established that it was at least possible to do what Brendan and his companions are reputed to have done.

His origins and fosterage

The mediaeval *Lives* of Brendan tell us that he was born by Tralee Bay in Co Kerry, in or about the year AD 484. He belonged to the *Ciarraighe Luachra* people. His parents are said to have had at least two other children, namely, Dromanigen, who became a bishop and a saint in Muskerry, Co Cork, and Briga, later abbess of a convent founded by Brendan at Annaghdown, on the shores of Lough Corrib in the county Galway. Brendan was baptised by St Erc at Tobar na Molt, near Ardfert. After a year or so, he was fostered out to St Ita, that illustrious woman of the Deci people, who had a convent at Killeedy in West Limerick. Ita nursed him with care and tenderness and all the nuns in the community were very fond of him because he was temperamentally a pleasant child. One day, St Ita asked him why he was looking so delighted and contented in himself. Brendan replied that it was because herself and the other nuns used to talk to him and hold him by the hand. (Parents and child-minders, please note!)

Brendan's education

St Erc took Brendan out of fosterage after a few years, say the *Lives*, and set him to the study of Latin and other subjects, as well as giving him work-experience in church affairs -Erc being a bishop as well as a saint. Brendan missed the pleasant time he had with the nuns, but his sister Briga, who had not yet entered the convent, used to visit him and comfort him.

In due time, Erc told him to move on for higher studies, and that Brendan did. On his way up the country he called on his foster-mother, St Ita, and told her that he was going to study for the priesthood. She was delighted at the news and gave him every encouragement and, wise woman that she was, she threw in a word of advice too, to the effect that he'd be as well to keep clear of convents for the most part, because people will talk!

At this time in Ireland – the early sixth century – it would have been normal for a lad aspiring to the priesthood and monastic life to get a basic grounding in the theory and practice of spirituality under St Enda in the Aran Islands. Having graduated from Aran – 'the novitiate of the Irish saints' – the next phase of study was to take theology at St Finian's highly rated monastic school at Clonard, Co Meath.

Having trained under Enda and Finian , Brendan is said to have spent some time with St Jarlath of Tuam. In fact, we are told that it was Brendan who helped Jarlath to settle there. The tradition relates that Jarlath was travelling one day and had occasion to change a wheel on his chariot, but Brendan told him not to worry any more about wheels because this spot was to be 'the place of his resurrection'. When Brendan eventually came back to his native Ciarraighe Luachra, the aged bishop Erc, as he had promised earlier, ordained him to the priesthood and soon afterwards Erc himself was gathered to his people.

Brendan's Travels

Even apart from the *Navigatio*, Brendan seems to have been regarded as a much travelled man. We find his name associated
with places in Ireland as near and as far apart as Ardfert,
Cloghane, Mt Brandon, Kilmaelkedar, the Blaskets, Valencia
Island – all in Kerry; with Inisdadroum in the Fergus-Shannon
estuary, Co Clare; with the Aran Islands, Tuam, Annaghdown,
and Clonfert in Co Galway; and with Inisglora off the Mullet
Peninsula in Co Mayo. And this list is not exhaustive.

Outside of Ireland Brendan is spoken of as being in Wales
and Brittany, while Scotland preserves his memory in a host of
places scattered across the mainland and islands, for example,
Cuil Bhrianainn (Brendan's Retreat) on the Garvellach islands,
and Kilbernie in Ayrshire. There are church sites called Cill
Bhrianainn in Lorne, Mull, Islay, Barra and St Kilda. Brendan
was patron of Boyndie in Banff and also patron of the island of
Bute. Natives of the latter island were at one time called
Brandans.

The *Lives* tell us that Brendan used to listen to an old sailor-
monk named Barind, whose stories enthused the younger man
for a yet wider missionfield. Barind recounted experiences of
journeys made by himself and other Irish monks to new and
lovely lands, not only north of Ireland but also south into the
warm climates of the Azores and possibly the West Indies.
Brendan figured that there were probably people out there in
the western ocean who had never heard the gospel message. He
would play his part in spreading the word. His prime ambition
was missionary.

The 'Navigatio' or Voyage of St Brendan

For long the Irish had believed in an earthly paradise, a
promised land, a *Tír na nÓg* or Land of the Young in the western
ocean, a sort of antechamber to the heavenly paradise. Nowhere
does the *Navigatio* say that Brendan was the first to go there. In
fact, it is quite clear from the texts that our saint and his companions were not so much 'discoverers' of that land, as visitors to it.

All along the route, on various islands, they meet lone hermits or whole communities of monks; and having made several vain attempts to get to the land of their dreams they eventually have to take on board an experienced pilot from one of these communities, who guides them through the fog banks to their ultimate goal.

Comparing Brendan's *Navigatio* with the *The Brendan Voyage* undertaken by Tim Severin, makes interesting reading. Severin follows what is known as the 'stepping-stone route' to North America, i.e. hopping from Ireland to the Hebrides, Faroes, Iceland, Greenland and Newfoundland. In the light of Severin's experiences on that journey, many parts of the *Navigatio* narrative came alive for him. He discovered the real existence of such places mentioned as the 'Paradise of Birds', the 'Island of Sheep', the 'Island of Smiths', and to the presence and antics of many gigantic and curious whales. All of these had previously been considered the fanciful creations of the author of the *Navigatio*.

Most interesting of all perhaps is the 'Island of Smiths'. Here the saga would seem to be giving a firsthand account of an underwater volcano erupting through the waves with all its dramatic fireworks and sulphur-stench. In the background is Iceland's famed volcanic mountain, Eyjafjallajokul, shooting fire into the air and swallowing it again. Little wonder that the terrified monks felt that they were coasting on the very brink of hell itself.

The Legend of Iasconius

Among the many and lovely legends recounted in the *Navigatio*, one of the best known is that of Iasconius. The story goes that at Easter time the monks landed on an island which was unusual to the extent that it had no harbour, no grass, no wood, and no sand on the shore. The monks spent the night in prayer and in the morning celebrated Mass. Everything went smoothly until it came to breakfast. After a cold night on the island, the monks decided on a cooked breakfast and to that end lit a fire and placed a cauldron on it for the purpose of boiling fish. The newly lighted fire blazed satisfactorily; the monks added more fuel, and with that, the island began to shake and move about like a wave of the sea. The terrified monks rushed to the boat where Brendan helped each aboard and as soon as the last monk was in they moved swiftly from the shore. It was then that Brendan explained to them that the island on which they had halted for bed and breakfast was nothing other than a huge whale, the largest of all the creatures that swim in the ocean. And the name of that fish is Iasconius.

The founding of Clonfert

The *Lives* of Brendan inform us that on his return from voyaging he founded a convent at Annaghdown, over which his sister Briga was abbess. Then, some time about AD 559 or 560, when he was seventy-seven years of age, Brendan was presented with a site for his most famous monastery, ever since known as Clonfert, 'the plain of wonders'.

His death and funeral

It was at the convent in Annaghdown that Brendan died on Sunday 16 May, some time in the 570s of the Christian era. After celebrating Mass, the account tells us, he felt that death was coming upon him. He instructed those present to keep his death secret in the locality until his body had been transported to Clonfert for burial, because this was to be 'his place of resurrection'. He then blessed those present and stepped inside the house, praying as he did so: 'Into your hands, O Lord, I commend my spirit; release me, O Lord, my God.' That same day he made his last great voyage into the unknown, having reached the ripe old age of perhaps ninety-three or ninety-four. He was buried with due rites and honour by his community at Clonfert, where, to this day, his grave is pointed out. It lies in front of the exquisite Irish Romanesque doorway of the twelfth-century cathedral, and slightly to the right of it.

St Cummian the Tall

The monastery at Clonfert evolved into a highly regarded seat of learning, so much so that when the Elizabethan occupiers of Ireland set about establishing a university here, their choice was narrowed down to Clonfert or Dublin. In the event they opted for Dublin and so Trinity College came to be. In its heyday, Clonfert is said to have had a community of 3,000. According to the *Lives*, Brendan chose as his successor, or *comharb*, one St Moinena, a man of noted learning and holiness; but Moinena pre-deceased Brendan in AD 570 or 571. The *Féilire* of St Aengus of Tallaght describes him as 'bishop and *comharb* of Brendan'. Commemorating his death under 8 March, the *Martyrology of Donegal*, among others, describes him as bishop of Cluain-Fearta-Brenainn. So, instead of St Moinena, it seems that Brendan's immediate successor was St Fintan Coragh (the Melodious), so named because he was an outstanding psalm-singer and choir master. The *Féilire* commemorates him and his two immediate successors thus:

Fintan the Melodious, Senach the Rough,
Colman, son of Comgall, the guileless,
Three great (spiritual) kings with warfare of valour,
One after the other in the abbey (of Clonfert).

St Cummian the Tall

The next abbot-bishop of Clonfert was the most distinguished scholar in the Ireland of his day, and indeed of the entire seventh century. He was known as Cummian Fota, Cummian the Tall. Besides Cummian Fota there are others of the same name, notably, Cummian the Fair, abbot of Iona and Cummian bishop-abbot of Bobbio in Italy. Having distinguished him from these others, we are still left with some difficulties. Is the Abbot of Clonfert to be identified as the author of the *Penitential of Cummian?* And is he also the Cummian who wrote the *Paschal Epistle,* concerning the dating of Easter? Nobody has conclusive answers to these questions. Mindful of that fact, we shall proceed on the basis of the learned Archbishop John Healy's opinions expressed in *Ireland's Ancient Schools and Scholars* as to the identity of the saint and his career.

Cummian's family background and education

If the tradition be authentic, Cummian had a shaky start in life. He was a foundling, and of the sept of the Eoghanach Lough Lein in the Killarney area. His parents are said to have abandoned him outside St Ita's convent at Killeedy in west Limerick. Finding him in a small *cummian* or basket, the sisters named him Cummian. By all accounts Cummian's mother was a lady to be reckoned with. She is said to have married four times and given birth to no less than six kings and six bishops. In later years she became a nun, lived to an advanced age, and died a saintly death.

Cummian himself had the good fortune to study at the famed school of Cork under the brilliant professor Colman Mac Ó Cluasaigh, a man who loved poetry and song. A lengthy *lorica* or protection prayer attributed to Cummian is preserved in the *Liber Hymnorum.* It invokes the protection of the Lord and his saints against the Yellow Plague which wrought havoc in Ireland in the mid-seventh century. The opening stanzas run:

God's blessing lead us, help us!
May Mary's Son veil us!
May we be under his safeguard tonight!
Whither we go may he guard us well!

Whether in rest or motion,
Whether sitting or standing.
The Lord of heaven against every strife,
This is the prayer that we will pray ...

Of Cummian the poet, Dr Healy says that 'we cannot say as much for his verses as for his theology,' and wryly adds, 'it is rarely, indeed, that theologians are good poets – they have too much sobriety of mind.' However, so great was the general reputation of St Cummian that he was compared to Pope St Gregory the Great, and at least one admirer thought him the only suitable successor to Gregory in the chair of Peter.

His involvement in 'The Paschal Controversy'

We don't know the exact date when Cummian became abbot and Bishop of Clonfert but it would seem to have been shortly after AD 620. His fame as a saint and scholar spread throughout Ireland and students flocked to the monastery. He appears to have taken a leading role at the National Synod of Magh Lene (close to Rahan, Co Offaly), held about AD 630. The main item on the agenda at that Synod was the burning issue of the day: the question of the right date for the celebration of Easter. This matter had been an irritant in the church in Ireland and Britain for some time as the old Roman system for calculating the date of Easter operating since Patrician times had been replaced in Rome by a new and more accurate one.

The assembly at Magh Lene decided to send delegates to Rome to observe when and how Easter was celebrated there. On their return home it was resolved to celebrate Easter on the same day with their 'mother the Church of Rome'. This was done, at least in the midlands and the south and east of Ireland, the area principally represented at the Synod of Magh Lene.

While that settled the controversy in those areas, the northern portion of Ireland held out against adopting the new system, chiefly because of the influence of the powerful monastery of Iona. It was probably at the request of those attending the Synod that Cummian, in or about AD 634, wrote his now famous *Paschal Epistle* to Segienus the Abbot of Iona, in an effort to get the Columban monasteries to conform. Though Cummian must have been well known and respected among the followers of Colmcille, the letter failed to produce results. A ninth-century copy of the *Epistle*, now preserved in the Library of St Gall, Switzerland, shows the Abbot of Clonfert to be a man of wide learning. And from his *Penitential*, which is preserved along with the *Epistle*, one can see that he was also a good moral theologian.

A *Penitential* can be described as a book of guidelines for letting the punishment fit the crime. It belongs to a genre of confessors' handbooks which evolved in Ireland in the sixth century and had an active life-span of about three hundred years, receiving widespread acceptance in Britain and the continent. Though often receiving a bad press from modern commentators, the *Penitentials* had a humanity about them that was frequently lacking in later times. Although firm and clear in their prescriptions, they gave due weight to the extenuating circumstances of a sin – ignorance, inadvertence, overwhelming feelings, and the like. Broadly speaking, their strategy was to establish the penitent in a healing process whereby the right virtue was cultivated to build up resistance to its opposing vices, e.g. cultivating moderation and abstinence in order to overcome gluttony and drunkenness, the practice of open-handed generosity as a means of overcoming avarice, wishing people well as a means of overcoming envy and hatred, self-control and practising sexual purity as a means of overcoming lust and adultery.

Several Irish *Penitentials* survive from mediaeval times, Cummian's being one of the best known. It contains little that is original but it is remarkable for the author's knowledge of the early Christian writers and of church history generally, and in particular the penitential stipulations of various church councils. On the issue of gluttony, Cummian invites the penitent to focus on St Luke's gospel, 'But take heed of yourselves lest your hearts be weighed down with dissipation and drunkenness and cares of this life, and that day come upon you suddenly like a snare; for it will come upon all who dwell upon the face of the whole earth' (Lk 21:34-5). By citing this gospel passage, Cummian shows his awareness that excessive eating and drinking is sinful because it dulls the mind and ultimately leads to further dissipation, so that one's life gets out of hand.

Cummian's death and mourning

Both Cummian and his professor, St Colman Mac Ó Cluasaigh, died in the same year. The *Annals of the Four Masters* record Cummian's death as taking place on 12 November, AD 661. Not long after, Colman Mac Ó Cluasaigh followed him to the grave, but not before first composing an elegy on the death of his illustrious pupil whose fame was so great that even the mention of his name in Rome itself would open many a door to the pilgrim.

The same annals preserve a portion of Colman's elegy. From the text it would seem that Cummian died in the Lower Shannon area (Luimneach) and that his body was conveyed by boat up the river to Clonfert where he was interred:

The Luimneach did not bear on its bosom,

of the race of Munster, into Leath Chuinn,

A corpse in a boat so precious as he,

as Cummian, son of Fiachna.

If any one went across the sea,

to sojourn at the seat of Gregory [Rome],

If from Ireland,

he requires no more than the mention of Cummian the Tall.

I sorrow after Cummian,

from the day that his shrine was covered;

My eyelids have been dropping tears;

I have not laughed, but mourned since the lamentation

at his barque.

St Ciarán of Clonmacnoise

In 1549, when a detachment of English soldiers came down from Athlone on a final pillaging expedition to the already plundered monastery of Clonmacnoise, the holy foundation had completed a lifespan of full a thousand years since that far-off day when the youthful and saintly Ciarán had chosen it as 'the place of his resurrection'. In the intervening millennium, its reputation was such that the student population numbered thousands, and were drawn from all over Europe. After Armagh it was the greatest monastic church in Ireland, and in learning and literature probably the greatest. Even in its present ruinous state it is our most poignant set of historical and archaeological remains.

Geographically Clonmacnoise stands on an oasis in the midst of vast boglands, on the eastern bank of the Shannon, about ten miles south of Athlone. With the Shannon running north-south and the ancient highway along the Esker Riada running east-west, this was the cross roads of Ireland.

St Ciarán, the founder, is known as Ciarán the Younger, to distinguish him from another St Kieran who had a monastic foundation at Saighir-Kieran on the Offaly-Tipperary border. Because his father was a craftsman – a carpenter it is said – the saint is known also as Ciarán Mac a' tSaoir, Ciarán son of the tradesman, a name which has been anglicised to MacIntyre or MacAteer. According to the *Lives*, the carpenter was a native of Larne, Co Antrim who married a Kerrywoman – both of them being refugees from their native sod and now settled around Fuerty, about three miles from Roscommon. They had five sons and three daughters, all of them solid in the faith, but the most outstanding of the lot was Ciarán.

According to early accounts of his life, he was baptised at Fuerty by Justus the Deacon. Ciarán received his early education from Justus, and in turn earned his keep by herding the cattle and doing other domestic and farm chores. Then, as now, the process of becoming a fully fledged monk usually involved training in a number of centres. Ciarán, having left Justus the Deacon, furthered his training at St Finnian's school at Clonard. He is presented to us as being on close terms with a number of fellow students, among them, Colmcille, Brendan the Navigator, Mobí, Ninnidh and Tighernagh of Clones. No doubt these, among others, benefited from the milk and milk products derived from the cow which Ciarán had brought with him to Clonard. This cow gave milk for many years and when it died, its hide was preserved in Clonmacnoise as a sacred relic to which healing properties were attributed.

'All you need is love'
The image of Ciarán created in the *Lives* is of a happy serious-minded young man who led an extremely ascetic life. He never passed a day without manual work for the benefit of the brethren. He was never idle. He slept on the bare ground with a stone for a pillow and never wore a soft garment next his skin. There was no saint more loved by his contemporaries. Even as I write, it is still true that along the Shannon there is no saint remembered with greater affection than he. So loved was he that a strange and thoroughly unChristian legend has it that the saints of Ireland prayed that he would die because they were so jealous of him!

As a person, he is presented as thoughtful, gentle, obliging, and generous-hearted. The quality of his gentleness is preserved in the quaint little story of the fox that tried to eat the leather cover of a manuscript. When hunted down, the clever little fellow took refuge under Ciarán's cloak, and ever after remained on in the monastery as a pet.

Ciarán's generosity knew no bounds, and students of every subject and generation will readily appreciate the story of

Ciarán giving his manuscript of St Matthew's gospel to St Ninnidh. It so happened that during study time, St Ninnidh did not have a copy of the gospel of Matthew, and nobody would lend him one as all the students were preparing for class. 'Did you try Ciarán?' said St Finnian. With that, the young monk went along and the generous Ciarán obliged even though he had his own lesson only half prepared. Next day in class it was obvious that our saint had only half the lesson on St Matthew's gospel, so some wag among the students nicknamed him 'Ciarán-half-Matthew'. St Finnian heard this, and in a prophetic reference to Ciarán's greatness, he said: 'Not Ciarán-half-Matthew but Ciarán-half-Ireland!'

It is also recounted in the *Lives* that in the absence of St Finnian his chair of learning was filled by the young Ciarán, and further that when the time came for Ciarán to move on from Clonard, the great Finnian offered to resign his post in favour of Ciarán. And no wonder, for in later years, St Cummian of Clonfert would number Ciarán among the 'early Fathers of the Irish church', and the renowned mediaeval abbot and poet Alcuin referred to him as 'the glory of the Irish nation.'

Despite Finnian's plea, however, Ciarán did move on, feeling the need to further his spiritual formation, and to that end set his face towards Aran of St Enda and spent some years there. That his spiritual master thought highly of his pupil is dramatically portrayed in the account of their parting at the beach in Killeany: 'O my brethren,' said Enda, as the tears streamed down his face, 'good reason have I to weep, for this day has our island … lost the flower and strength of religious observance.'

Ciarán the Founder
At the end of his training in Aran, he set out with a dozen companions, in the spirit of Jesus and the apostles. He visited St Senan's monastery on Scattery Island at the mouth of the Shannon, then pushed upstream, making a foundation first at Inis Ciarán and later at Hare Island in Lough Ree, in the upper reaches of the river. He is said to have stayed a little over three

years on Hare Island before moving further south to a spot called *Ard Tiprait,* the Height of the Well; and there, on *Clúain-moccu-Nóis,* the meadow of the race of Nós, he settled. According to his *Life,* it was Saturday, 3 January. The year is uncertain: the annals vary between AD 545 and 549, but it was certainly within that fourth decade of the century. Here he and eight companions built a little wooden church and whatever other domestic buildings were necessary.

When they were building the wooden framework for the first church, it happened that Diarmuid O Carroll, a refugee prince, together with some companions was present. Diarmuid, sturdy young man that he was, helped Ciarán in sinking the first corner-post. Out of respect and reverence for Ciarán he placed his own hand beneath that of Ciarán, thus taking the shock of the blows involved in sinking the pole. Ciarán said to him: 'Though your companions today are few, tomorrow you will be High King of Ireland.' And so indeed he was. King Tuathal Maelgarbh, great grandson of Niall of the Nine Hostages, who had a warrant out for the life of Diarmuid, was killed; and as the refugee at Clonmacnoise was the heir to the throne, he took up his office without opposition.

Ciarán lived only a very short time after making the foundation; the earliest *Life* says that it was as little as one year. The cause of his death was the *Buidhe Chonaill,* the Yellow Plague. He was still a young man in his thirties on that Saturday in September when death overtook him, but we cannot say whether or not the age of thirty three, given by his biographer, is chronologically correct or simply symbolic of the age of Christ. That first *Life* describes how Ciarán asked to be taken out of his cell into the open air. When he grew weaker the monks brought him into the *Eaglais Bheag* – the first little church – where he had prayed so much. The skin on which he used to sleep was spread out on the ground and the dying saint was placed upon it. He requested to be left alone with his *anam-chara* and fellow student at Clonard, St Kevin of Glendalough. Kevin blessed water and sprinkled it about and then gave Holy Communion to Ciarán. In turn, Ciarán gave Kevin his bell, the symbol of monastic rule. Having blessed his people and clergy he breathed his last. From that day to this, over fourteen and a half centuries, the feast of Ciarán is celebrated on 9 September each year. Even as early as the year AD 800, St Aengus of Tallaght refers to the large crowds coming by land, and to the heavy shipping traffic on the Shannon on that day.

The secret of Clonmacnoise

Clonmacnoise was unique in Ireland in that it was not under the sway of any particular tribe. This factor allowed for an independence, freedom and largeness of vision not generally enjoyed by other religious establishments. One commentator describes Ciarán's monastery as more or less the equivalent of a national seminary. Its monks and scholars came from all over the country, and its abbots likewise, the first four being, in turn, from Connacht, Leinster, Ulster and Munster.

The *Eaglais Bheag,* where the saint died, became a sacred spot. It was the centre of holiness in Clonmacnoise. St Adomnán of Iona says that after the convention of Drumceat in 575 Colmcille himself paid a visit to Clonmacnoise and the grave of his erstwhile schoolmate. He took some of the holy soil to bring back to Iona but threw it into the sea during a storm to calm the waves. Relics of Ciarán include the *Imda Chiaráin,* or cow-skin couch on which he died. (This was the hide of the dun cow which Ciarán had brought with him to Clonard.) It was considered to have curative properties and sick people would lie in it in the hope of recovery. His body was buried in the *Eaglais Bheag,* now demolished, but the grave is thought to be close by the southern wall of *Teampall Chiaráin.* The graveyard in Clonmacnoise was considered as sacred a burial place as any in Rome. Many of the noblest families sought burial rights there since it was popularly believed that Ciarán brought to heaven the souls of all buried in that holy ground. This is the reference in Ó Gillan's poem translated by T. W. Rollston:

In a quiet watered land, a land of roses,
Stands St Kieran's city fair;
And the warriors of Erin in their famous generation
Slumber there.
…
There they laid to rest the seven Kings of Tara
There the sons of Cairbre sleep –
Battle-banner of the Gael, that in Kieran's plain of crosses,
Now their final hosting keep.

St Ninnidh

The calendar of Irish saints begins with a first flowering of St Patrick and his contemporaries and some who preceded him. The following generation or two provide fewer saints, though among them is the luminous Brigid of Kildare. Then, a century or so after Patrick, Ireland bursts into bloom in a dazzling summertime of holiness with Finnian, Comgall, Mobí, Ciarán, Brendan, Ita, Kevin, Cainnech, Tighernagh, Carthage – the list is endless.

It was at this time of flowering that the entire Erne basin became a sort of Mecca for hermits, monks, and monastic communities. The thought of Devenish, Cleenish and White Island is enough to jog the memory. There is a host of ancient sites on the islands and shores of the Lough, each with a story to tell. In Lower Lough Erne lies Inismacsaint, the island where Ninnidh settled. Little is known about him, but his status in mediaeval times was such as to have him listed among the Twelve Apostles of Ireland, a hall of fame reputed to have been chosen from among St Finnian's most outstanding disciples. The twelve apostles include Ciarán of Saighir, Ciarán of Clonmacnoise, Colmcille of Derry, Brendan of Birr, Brendan of Clonfert, Colmán of Terryglass, Molaise of Devenish, Cainnech of Kilkenny, Ruadan of Lorrha, Mobí of Glasnevin, Sínell of Cleenish, and Ninnidh of Inismacsaint. While all were supposed to have studied under Finnian it is evident from closer analysis that such was impossible, considering the different times in which they lived. However, taking them as a group, they are among the most significant of the great monastic saints and founders in early Christian Ireland.

After training in Aran and Clonard, Ninnidh found his dream spot in Inismacsaint, a small island about half a mile off the western shore of Lower Lough Erne adjacent to Derrygonnelly. Here he made a monastic foundation. In his quest for God he also made use of a little hermitage on the slopes of Knockninny near Derrylin. (Incidentally, the name Inismacsaint has nothing to do with saints. It is one of those unfortunate anglicisations dating from the Ordinance Survey in the mid-nineteenth century. The original name is *Inis Maige Samh*, meaning, perhaps, the flat island of the sorrel or the flat peaceful island).

Ninnidh's monastery would not have been striking. Like virtually all sixth-century monasteries it was poor. Its architecture would have conformed to the accepted pattern of other early Christian monastic settlements in Ireland: a few central buildings such as a church and a dining hall, usually of wood with thatched or shingled roof; around them the cells of monks, with a retaining wall around the lot. This arrangement was known as the laura system; it was based on Egyptian prototypes. As well as those in vows or orders, the monastic community also included lay workers and students. In a large foundation these could be quite numerous so that, as the settlement evolved over the years, it took on the proportions of a village or small town. In fact many modern Irish towns have their origin in such settlements as these, Roscrea, Kells, and Cork being prime examples.

The regime in all Irish Celtic monasteries was essentially the same: prayer, study, fasting and manual labour. The prayer was based on the Bible. So, too, was much of the study, although other subjects such as theology, church history, astronomy, geography, Latin, folklore, and sometimes Greek, were also included in the curriculum. Other activities included farming, copying and illuminating manuscripts, artistic and practical work in metal, wood and stone.

The Bible was the chief subject of study, especially the psalms and the life of our Lord. When an Irish youngster of the

sixth century considered a monastic vocation, his first step was
to seek the guidance of some holy cleric. This was in keeping
with the Gaelic custom of fosterage. The cleric, as well as instructing him in the ways of the gospel, also taught him how to
read and write the Latin language. This prepared him for Bible
study. If he had not reached that level when entering a
monastery, his first task was to learn to read the psalms and
learn the entire one hundred and fifty of them by heart. 'There
are three enemies attacking me,' said St Mael Ruan of Tallaght,
'my eyes, my tongue and my thoughts; the psalms restrain them
all.'

The manual labour was not an optional extra, nor was it de-
vised as penitential exercise. It was necessary if the monks were
to stave off starvation. Despite the fact that the monks lived simply, the matter of maintaining an adequate food supply was an
on-going task. Bread, fish, and eggs, together with milk and
milk products were all part of the monastic diet. Meat was
sometimes available, while fresh vegetables were in short supply and almost non-existent in winter. Indeed, one of the attrac-
tions of the Erne must have been the ready supply of eggs and
fish, and an occasional feast from the hunt.

Fasting and penance were encouraged as a means of achiev-
ing clarity of mind and keeping one's sexual urges under control. Fasting from food was not the only kind of penance prac-
tised; denial of sleep, interruption of sleep, endurance of cold,
were all part and parcel of a growing mastery over oneself. As
the monastic tradition evolved, some of the more exotic and exceptional forms of penance gained a notoriety in the tradition
that the facts hardly warranted. We note references to standing
up to one's neck in a cold lake, or praying the Cross-Vigil with
outstretched arms for periods of time beyond normal human endurance.

Ninnidh is spoken of as abbot, doctor (teacher) and bishop. It
seems that as well as his island monastery he had responsibility
for a territory stretching south of Upper Lough Erne and west to
Donegal Bay. He is not to be confused with an earlier saint of the

same name who is said to have been a friend and confidant of St Brigid, and to have attended her at her death.

Ninnidh died around the middle of the sixth century. His feast is commemorated on 18 January in the eighth-century *Martyrology of Tallaght*, and also by seventeenth-century anti-quary and scribe, Dubhaltachd McFirbis. His bell was long pre-served as a precious relic ornamented with silver and gold. It was used as a guarantee of trust and truth in much the same fashion as the Bible is used in law courts today.

The Celtic monastery at Inismacsaint seems to have survived down to the twelfth century and the little church became a parish church within the diocese of Clogher. As with most Celtic monasteries, the material remains are meagre. A ruined church, a 13-foot stone cross, some mounds of earth where monastic cells once stood, and the remains of a rampart enclosing what seems to have been a monastic settlement of considerable size and importance. A late medieval window which had survived the ravages of centuries was removed from the church and, as far as I know, inserted into a Protestant church in the neighbour-hood.

Near the modern town of Derrylin is Knockninny – St Ninnidh's Hill – and the saint's holy well. Knockninny, which is over 600 feet high, seems to have been a place of considerable importance in civilian life as it was the seat of the powerful McGuire family, one of whom, Conor McGuire, Baron of Inniskillen, suffered martyrdom for the Catholic faith at Tyburn Hill, London in AD 1645, a salutary reminder that following the way of Jesus is a dangerous occupation in any age, ours being no exception.

Although our knowledge of his life is skimpy enough, we know that St Ninnidh, in the days of his youth, made choices to follow the way of Jesus. These choices were not easily or lightly made: girls were as lovely then as now, and wealth and status every bit as tempting. On his remote island or bleak hill-top he allowed nothing and nobody to distract him from the pursuit of loving God who has become visible in our world through Christ

Jesus Our Lord. The gospel is no different in our time. And what St Columbanus wrote for his monks half a century after St Ninnidh's death, has a strong message for humankind in every generation:

Remember, man, what you are,
and what one day you shall be.
For what you are,
you are but for an instant;
while what you shall be,
you shall be forever.
Win now in the fleeting moment of time
what you shall possess for eternity.
The rewards to come are indeed such
that they should induce you to triumph
over the hardships of the Godly life.
Follow realities,
not the pleasant likeness in the pool,
not the alluring riches of the dream
Sell your vices
and buy eternal life.

St Ita

At Templeglantin church, on the main Limerick-Tralee road, is a statue of St Ita, portraying her as a lovely young woman who, in my native Sliabh Luachra, would be described as *toslach:* a sturdy well-formed young damsel. It chimes with my own impression of her – an outer loveliness reflecting an inner goodness of heart, a goodness that marked her in youth, maturity and old age. In her origins, she is generally understood to be a scion of the *Dési* people of mid-Munster, and a native of what is now Co Waterford.

Vocation

A marriage arrangement with a nobleman was agreed by Ita's father but the spirited young lady resisted on the plea that she had consecrated her entire life to God. The father was less than pleased, furious in fact. Ita then explained to her mother the nature of the vocation she had in mind. It was still the early days of Christianity in Ireland and many people did not appreciate the idea of consecrating one's life entirely to Jesus Christ, and having none but him as one's chief and only love. When the mother had understood the situation more fully she put the case again to her husband but failed to move him towards a change of heart.

Ita had her own approach to the crisis: she fasted and prayed for three days and three nights. During this time, she was tempted to abandon her sacred project, but managed to resist every strategy of the tempter. At the end of her ordeal of fast, prayer and temptation, the father had come to a new realisation of what his wonderful daughter had in mind. He not only told her that she was free to take up her new life, but he encouraged her to do so in whatever place she might select. Having thus resolved the family tensions which had arisen, Ita then presented herself before the leader of a little church in the *Dési* country, consecrated her life through a vow of virginity, and received the veil, that is, a simple headdress symbolic of such consecration.

Foundation

Trusting herself to the providence of God, Ita set out to find a suitable place in which to settle. It is more than likely that she lived for a time in more than one location and acquired some disciples before finally coming to the place of her resurrection. According to the *Lives*, of which there are three, an angel facilitated them in finding that spot. It fell within that territory of the Uí Conaill, a branch of the Uí Fidgente, who occupied the western end of the Golden Vale south of Newcastlewest, towards the borders of Duhallow, in Co Cork. (The Uí Conaill name survives in the present baronies of Upper and Lower Connello, but the site chosen for Ita's convent is in the barony of Glenquin.) The local chieftain of the Uí-Connaill, with the approval of his people, granted her the land needed for her foundation. In fact he wished to give her much more than she required but Ita, wishing to remain poor for Christ's sake, was satisfied with a few acres suitable to grow vegetables for herself and the community. Events took their usual course and local young ladies, inspired by Ita and her companions, petitioned to join the community, so that the convent at Killeedy grew in numbers and status under this courageous woman on fire with the love of God.

Thirsting for God

The *Martyrology of Donegal* preserves a tradition about the saint that 'Deirdre was her first name'. However, because of her thirst for God, she was called Íota, i.e. 'parching thirst'. There are many variations of the name: Íte, Ita , Ida, Ide, Idea, Itha, Ytha, Ithey, Issey. In the Irish tradition, when a saint was particularly dear to people, they tended to prefix the name with *mo*, my, as exemplified in further versions of Ita's name: Mite, Mida, Midea, Mide, and in the West Limerick Parish of Kilmeedy, i.e. Cill mo Íde, church of my Ita.

The old Gaelic name for the convent was *Cluain-credal,* a term of uncertain meaning – 'the Nuns' Retreat,' 'the Meadow of Devotion,' or 'Holy Meadow' are possible translations – but the foundation is best known today, and for long centuries past, as *Cell-Íte* or Killeedy, the Church of St Ita. It lies about eight kilometres south of Newcastlewest with the mountainous regions of Sliabh Luachra rising ahead of it. Little is known of the later history of *Cluain-credal,* but it is thought to have become a monastery of men in the course of time.

Foster-mother of the saints

The three surviving *Lives* of Ita are thought to draw on an earlier one, perhaps as early as the middle of the seventh century. According to the *Lives,* she is credited with many gifts: prophecy, healing, exorcism, mind-reading, second sight, raising the dead, communion with the angels of God, and more besides. Her deep devotion to the Holy Trinity is stressed, and in her little desert retreat away from the convent, she's pictured as spending her time quietly contemplate the mystery of the Holy Trinity.

Ita is known as the Foster-mother of the saints of Ireland. Among those said to have been fostered by her are, Brendan the Navigator, Cummian Fota of Clonfert, and the gentle and loving St Molua. It is said that when Brendan was a year old, Bishop Erc placed him in the care of Ita at Killeedy. There he remained for five years. He always looked on St Ita as a mother; he consulted her in difficulties because 'she was prudent in word and work, sweet and winning in her address, but constant of mind and firm of purpose'. The saints mentioned here are but a very small number of those who are said to have come to Killeedy for advice and direction from the wise woman of the *Dési,* the 'Brigid of Munster' as she is designated.

Ita was a woman of deep compassion. Illustrations of it abound. There is, for example, the story of the man who killed his brother. The murderer was condemned to death by the chief of the Uí Conaill, but Ita felt for the poor mother who had lost one son tragically and now was about to lose the other. Prompted by the double motive of comforting the mother and giving the erring son an opportunity for repentance, Ita petitioned the chief on behalf of the condemned man, offering to be guarantor for his future good conduct. The man was reprieved. Ita's wisdom now showed itself. The man would have to do penance, but Ita persuaded the chief to postpone the imposition of penance for a cooling off period, so that the man might come to his penance in a willing frame of mind rather than do it sullenly under compulsion.

A further illustration of Ita's compassion recounted in the *Lives* relates to an incident in the life of one of her nuns. Though there is no direct reference to what the incident was, it would seem that the nun, in a moment of weakness, got involved with a man and became pregnant. Furthermore, she denied any wrongdoing, but Ita had knowledge of it and had her dismissed from the convent. The poor nun had gone 'on the *sácrán*' and ended up as the slave of a magician in Connacht. Ita, through her gift of second sight, was aware of this and sent word to St Brendan in Clonfert to track her down and to get the king of Connacht to arrange for her freedom. Brendan ensured that the nun, together with a daughter, were sent back to Killeedy, where Ita received both mother and daughter not only with compassion but with real joy. The mother did due penance and thereafter lived blamelessly until her death.

Intercession for the dead

When an uncle of Ita died in the *Dési* country she summoned his eight sons to her convent and told them that all was not well with him on the other side of the grave. Because of his sins in this life he was in hell. (In early Christian Irish theology, the concept of 'hell' was not necessarily a place of eternal punishment; it was more akin to purgatory, but difficult to get out of.) Ita told these eight first cousins of hers that if they were prepared to give

food and light to the poor each day for a year, things could
change. This they undertook to do. At the end of the year they
returned and she had good news: the father was in much better
circumstances but still in need. For the next year the young men
were to repeat the generosity of the previous one. On completion of the second year, Ita told them that he was released from
hell but that he had no clothes, for the simple reason that during
his earthly life he had failed to clothe the poor in Christ's name.
At the end of the third year Ita told them that their father now
enjoyed rest, and that this condition had been achieved for him
through their alms and her prayers, but above all through the
mercy of God. She then further admonished the cousins to
behave themselves, to live decently and practise self-restraint,
because it was for lack of these virtues that their father had suffered.

Suffering and death

Although Ita lived to a ripe old age, she is said to have secretly
suffered a martyrdom from an affliction which, according to
some scholars at least, may have been a terrible cancer.
Whatever it was, it is presented as a great black stag-beetle eating into her side. When news of her approaching death spread
abroad, clergy and laity, high and low, came to pay their re-
spects. Before her departure from this life she invoked a blessing
on the people of Uí Conaill, who in turn adopted her as their
patron saint. As she lived, so she died, praying to the Holy
Trinity. Virtually all sources agree on 15 January as the actual
day of her death; the year is more problematic, but it is likely to
have been in or about AD 570. She was buried at her own convent in Killeedy.

The name and fame of Ita spread at home and abroad. She is
invoked in the litany of the saints in the eighth-century *Tallaght
(Stowe) Missal*. Her name is preserved in Rosmead (Co
Westmeath), as well as in several churches of Cornwall. And
Alcuin, the renowned educationalist in the Carolingian
Renaissance of the late eighth century, mentions her in one of his

poems. But to the people of the *Dési* and the south she will always remain the darling of Munster.

St Kevin

It is disappointing to go to the source material on many of the early Irish saints and discover the paucity of historical data. This is the situation even with such a prominent saint as Kevin, or *Coemgen*, of Glendalough. That he existed is beyond doubt. There is substantial agreement on when and where he lived. Five versions of his *Life*, some in Latin, some in Irish, are preserved in Brussels, Oxford and Dublin, respectively. The earliest *Life* – a Latin version – dates from about the tenth or eleventh century and, in common with the later four, it is sadly deficient in historical content. Side by side with this historical poverty is a wealth of tradition, lore and legend, both in regard to the saint himself and to his famous monastic site at Glendalough, Co Wicklow.

Early life
In the *Lives*, the saint is presented as being of royal Leinster stock on both sides of the family, but as this is a hagiographical convention, one cannot be sure. At an early age he was fostered out to St Petroc, a monk of Padstowe in Cornwall, who was then pursuing scripture studies in Ireland. After twelve years formation under him, Kevin underwent further training under three holy men, Eoghan, Lochan and Enna, at their little monastic settlement at Kilnamanagh, the suggested location of which is north-east of Rathdrum, also in Co Wicklow. He was ordained to the priesthood by a bishop Lughaí. He is reputed to have been a wonderful lover of nature, comfortable in the company of bird and beast, sensitive to their songs and sounds, a devotee of deep solitude, fiercely ascetic, given to prayerful vigils under the open canopy of the heavens and, like his siblings, male and

64

female, he is said to have been remarkable for holiness and physical beauty.

It was this latter characteristic that gave rise to the story of Kevin's encounter with an attractive and persistent young lady who became enamoured of the youth. A version of the tale, much different from the original, and popularised by Zozimus, the Dublin balladeer, gives her the name Kathleen. Zozimus claims in his entertaining doggerel verses that Kevin summarily disposed of the poor girl in most unsaintly fashion:

He threw her right into the lake

And she sank right down to the bottom.

The account given in the early *Lives* is somewhat less dramatic and certainly more Christian. The story goes that a young lady cultivated Kevin's friendship in the hope of winning his heart. The innocent Kevin, not recognising the hidden agenda, returned the friendship. One day, however, when she managed to meet him on his own, she revealed her real intentions and, literally, assaulted him with kisses. Kevin tried to maintain his composure, and not only resisted all the blandishments of the besotted girl, but flung himself into a clump of nettles to cool any desires he might have had. And to cool down his attacker, he grabbed a bunch of the burning nettles and administered them vigorously to her, so that, as the author of the *Life* philosophically comments: 'The fire without put out the fire within.' The upshot of the entire encounter was that Kathleen repented of her action, asked pardon of God and Kevin, and became a nun.

The City of St Kevin
If Kevin loved solitude then his choice of Glendalough was a truly inspired one. Even today, with its interpretative centre and tourist traffic, it retains a calm and charm of rare quality. A hundred years ago bishop John Healy, author of *Ireland's Ancient Schools and Scholars*, wrote: 'Glendalough – the valley of the two lakes – is, for a religious and cultivated mind, one of the most interesting spots in Ireland. Nature has made it wild and beautiful; religion has hallowed its scenery with the holiest associations;

the genius of song has lit up its dark lakes and mountains with all the radiance of romance. It is one of those places the very sight of which raises the mind from mean and sordid thoughts to the contemplation of what is beautiful and good.' Here Kevin, the Fair-begotten one, lived without fire or roof, but to an unusual degree attended by bird and beast in the surrounding wilderness.

The monastic site at Glendlough is set deep among the Wicklow hills. Mountains of over 2,000 feet surround the narrow valley in which it is situated except for an opening towards the level ground on the banks of the Avonmore river. Glendalough is protected from the north winds by the Brockagh and Comderry hills but the peaks of Derrybawn and Lugduff to the south exclude the sunshine. It was probably on the inhospitable slopes of Lugduff that the founder of the monastery first settled: above his head a lofty and precipitous cliff, at his feet the dark waters of the upper of two lakes from which the place name *Gleann dá Loch*, valley of the two lakes, is derived.

Díseart Coemghen, or Kevin's Desert, is the name now given to this area of the valley where the chief remaining ruins are Reefert Church and Temple-na-Skellig, together with a scatter of low stone crosses, the footings of St Kevin's Cell, and some other amorphous archaeological remains. It is likely that, with the increase of disciples, this site proved too restrictive. Whether this be the reason or not, the monastery was relocated a little further down the valley in the delta 'where,' as the *Life* puts it, 'two sparkling rivers meet'. The rivers still sparkle, the Glendasan and the Glenalo. They come together in the middle of the valley to form the Glendalough River and flow on to join the Avonmore at Laragh. At the place of their first confluence stands what has long been called The Monastic City of St Kevin.

Legends galore

During his time in Glendalough, Kevin is said to have spent an hour each night in the cold lake waters. During this hour he was tormented by the presence of a menacing monster that used to swim around him. Then God sent an angel to Glendalough on a three-fold mission: to reduce Kevin's penances, to drive away the monster, and to warm up the lake. The angel came each night and supervised the implementation of all three tasks.

Legends abound concerning Kevin's relationship with bird and beast. Perhaps the best known is the story of Kevin praying the Cross Vigil – hands stretched out in the form of a cross – when a little bird, not only perched on his hand but built a nest and laid her eggs there. Not wanting to disturb the little bird, Kevin kept his hands outstretched until the little ones were hatched out and had flown away! On another occasion when Kevin was at prayer beneath a tree, a wild boar, being pursued by the hounds of Brandubh, king of Leinster, rushed into Kevin's cell but the pursuing dogs stopped short at the door and sat down. Meanwhile, Kevin remained at prayer while the birds of the air, comfortably perched on his head and shoulders, or flying round about him, continued to warble and sing their songs of praise. Even the rustle of the very leaves of the trees in Glendalough was thought to be a sweet music chanted to ease the great penances of the saint.

It is related that at one time in his life Kevin set out on pilgrimage. He had hardly reached Dublin when a holy hermit named Garbán accosted him and said: 'O servant of God, where are you going? It is better for you to remain in one spot, serving the Lord, than to go about from place to place, in your old age; for you have heard that no bird, while flying, can hatch her eggs.' Kevin returned to base and St Garbán stayed with him as a disciple. This legend is probably included to discourage monks from wandering all over the place in the name of pilgrimage. The *Life* recording this incident is probably of tenth or eleventh century date because it comments that Dublin of that time was 'a powerful and warlike city, where ever dwell men fierce in battle, and skilful in handling fleets' – surely a reference to the Vikings.

Another good reason for not going on pilgrimage is to have the care of a little baby. This circumstance arose when Kevin was asked to care for Foelán, the child of a broken marriage. The saint joyfully undertook the fosterage and, wonder of wonders, to supply nourishment for the baby a doe came down from the mountain each day and waited until she had been milked by one of the monks, so that the child blossomed and grew to man's estate, until he ultimately inherited the chiefdom of his father.

Two favourite disciples of Kevin were St Berach, later of Termonbarry on the Shannon, and Mocherog, a Briton, and founder of a church at Delgany; it was from him that Kevin is said to have received the Viaticum, the body and blood of Christ, shortly before his death. Among other friends mentioned in the *Lives* is Ciarán of Clonmacnoise after whom is named a chapel now among the ruins of the monastic city. Shortly after the death of Ciarán, Kevin, together with Colmcille, Comgall of Bangor and Canice of Aghabo and Kilkenny, attended a conference on the Hill of Uisneach, and the *Lives* say that a very big crowd of people came there just to see Colmcille. Afterwards, Kevin is said to have returned to Glendalough and lived out the remaining sixty years of his life. The *Annals of Ulster* give his death as occurring on 3 June 618, when he was 120 years old!

Down the road of time
Kevin is credited with having written a rule, but if he did, it is no longer extant. The monastery continued to expand after his death and enjoyed a high reputation for learning and piety. It also had several daughter houses forming a *parouchia* or federation with the original foundation. While Kevin himself would not seem to have been ordained bishop, Glendalough is a diocese from time immemorial and in mediaeval times saw itself ranking next to Kildare in importance.

Because of its reputation, Glendalough was looked upon as a place of importance in life and in death. It was there at Reefert church (*Rígh Fearta*, the royal cemetery), that the local O'Toole kings found their last resting place, and it was Lawrence, a member of that same Clann who initiated a new era of renewal and spiritual development making Glendalough famous in another age.

St Adomnán

The ninth Abbot of Iona, Adomnán by name, was an extraordinarily gifted man. In his own day and for long afterwards he seems to have been perceived as worthy of much the same status and veneration accorded to St Colmcille. By a strange quirk of fate, it may have been sheer fascination with Adomnán's *Life of Colmcille* that caused later generations to overlook the claim to fame of the author himself.

Adomnán was a man of action, a man of letters and a man of God. His ability and versatility were such as to combine a deep religious life with such varied activities as administrative work in the monastery and historical and literary research in the *scriptorium,* together with diplomacy and statesmanship on the international stage in both civil and religious affairs.

Early years

His family, who were of the Cinél Conaill in modern Co Donegal, equalled if not exceeded in nobility that of St Colmcille, of whom he was a first cousin thrice removed. He was born about AD 624, just a generation after the death of Colmcille. The location is uncertain but it was probably a little south of the Inishowen peninsula. 'It was in my youth,' he says, 'that a very old man called Ferreol, a servant of Christ, who is buried in Drumhome, told me of a glorious vision which he saw, when fishing in the valley of the Finn, on the night of Columba's death.' It is probable that at an early age he joined one of Colmcille's communities in that area, possibly Drumhome or Raphoe.

Equally uncertain are the date and circumstances of his arrival

on Iona. What we do know is that on the death of Abbot Fáilbhe
of Iona in 679, Adomnán was elected abbot of that monastery
and remained in office until his death in 704. It is in the quarter
of a century of his abbotship that we discover him to be an ur-
bane gentleman and stylist in the Latin language, a biblical
scholar, a historian, grammarian, geographer. All-round he was
a fine human being, charitable and obliging, humble and ascetic.
It is no surprise to find a person of this calibre elected superior
general of the Columban Order which then comprised the
largest federation of houses in the combined regions of Ireland
and Britain.

The man of letters

There is general agreement with the historian Bishop Reeves
that Adomnán's *Life of Colmcille* is 'perhaps the most valuable
monument of the Irish church which has escaped the ravages of
time.' To Thurneysen it is the 'pearl' of Irish hagiography. And
Kathleen Hughes warns its critics: 'To claim that the *Life* is a
purely artificial creation without regard to Columban tradition
would be perverse.' Adomnán himself says that he wrote at the
request of the community and that he is narrating 'what has
been handed down in the consistent tradition of our elders,
trustworthy and discerning men, setting down in all candour
the facts I have been able to find written in books before my
time, and those which, in response to my careful inquiries, have
been related to me orally by certain well-informed, trustworthy
old men, who spoke from personal knowledge and conviction.'

The predominant influence in Adomnán's Latinity is the
Bible, but it is also suggested that it bears traces of the influence
of the Latin *Life of St Anthony the Abbot*, and among others,
Sulpicius Severus, Gregory the Great, Virgil, Juvencus. From an
Irish standpoint the *Life of St Colmcille* is the most significant of
the four seventh-century works that have survived, the others
being Cogitosus' *Life of St Brigid*, written at the request of the
Kildare community, Muirchú's *Life of Patrick*, written by order of
Aed, Bishop of Sletty, and another *Life of Patrick* written by
Tírechán, a cleric and disciple of St Ultan of Ardbraccan.

'Concerning the Holy Places'

The second most important of Adomnán's surviving books is *De Locis Sanctis,* Concerning the Holy Places. On completion of this work he presented it to his friend and pupil, King Aldfrith of Northumbria, and in time it became the basis of the Venerable Bede's own work on the same subject. What occasioned Adomnán's writing of this book was the shipwreck of the Gaulish (French) Bishop Arculf who had been driven off course on his return voyage from the Holy Land. Adomnán not only gave him the hospitality of Iona but used the occasion to take copious notes on Arculf's personal observations and experience of those places so dear to Christians at all times. *De Locis Sanctis,* the book compiled from these notes, is one of the earliest accounts of a Western European visiting the the Holy Land and the Near East. Besides, it is the only extant account from the late seventh century, a time when the political life of the area was in ferment. For example, when Adomnán was in his teens Jerusalem and Alexandria fell to Islam; while in his mid twenties Islam took the imperial naval base of Cyprus and by the time he reached fifty Constantinople, the capital of the Byzantine Empire, was regularly under threat from the Muslim advance.

The book reflects the keenness of Arculf's observations and Adomnán's inquiring mind and meticulous chronicling. The Gaulish bishop had travelled widely as well as spending nine months based in Jerusalem during which time he visited the various holy sites both in the city itself and in the country round about. Adomnán questioned him closely on fifty-nine different aspects of his observations, on topics such as the Church of the Holy Sepulchre, the place of the Ascension, the Grotto on the Mount of Olives, the lance that pierced Christ's side and the shroud that wrapped his dead body, the Church of Mary's Dormitian and Marian iconography. Adomnán further inquired about the Oak of Mambre, Gilgal, the tombs of David, Rachel, and St Jerome, the place of Jesus' baptism in the Jordan, the source of the Jordan, the colour of the Jordan, the Dead Sea, the Sea of Galilee, the well of Samaria, the site associated with the feeding of the five thousand. Also included were inquiries concerning the nature of the terrain between Jerusalem and Caesarea, the nature of the pine forests from which wood was brought by camels to Jerusalem, together with questions relating to altitudes, vineyards, crops, Bethlehem, Nazareth, Caphernaum, Thabor, Damascus, Tyre, Constantinople, Alexandria; and about the river Nile and its crocodiles, which creatures he describes as 'aquatic four-footed beasts, not very large, but very voracious'. And more besides!

The 'Visions' and the 'Law'

Several other works are attributed to the pen of Adomnán but they are clearly of a later date. Notable among these is the *Fís Adamnáin* or Visions of Adomnán, a highly imaginative work of tenth or eleventh century date. The 'visions' of the title were colourful and fantastical visions of heaven and hell purported to have been seen by Adomnán, but the document also contains many insights into the social and religious milieu of the time. As a piece of Irish 'vision literature' it is second only to the Vision of Fursa, which is thought to have provided the inspiration for Dante's *Inferno*.

We turn next to a tract known as *The Law of Adomnán (Cáin Adamnáin)*. It is essentially an historical document dating from about the ninth century but embodying material from much earlier date, and concerns an assembly thought to have met at Leiter, near Birr, Co Offaly in 697. The assembly was impressive: a gathering of forty-eight kings and thirty-nine churchmen from all over Ireland. Among these latter were the powerful abbots of such great monasteries as Armagh, Clonard, Clonmacnoise, and Iona. At seventy-three Adomnán, Abbot of Iona, still full of energy and apostolic zeal, travelled the arduous journey by sea and land to be at that meeting, and there he had enacted the 'Law of the Innocents,' one of the most significant and enduring pieces of legislation to be adopted by civil and religious authorities in the Ireland of that time. The law was primarily directed at the amelioration of the condition of women within society by exempting them from military service. It also reached out to protect non-combatants in war situations and enacted severe punishments and compensations for killing women, children and clerical students.

The ecclesiastical diplomat

The controversy over the appropriate system for calculating the date of Easter raged all through Adomnán's life, and although he expended considerable time, energy and diplomacy on the subject, he died without seeing it fully resolved. True, he had considerable success among most of his Irish subjects, but his home community on Iona proved intractable. They refused to depart from the old Roman system, inherited from their founder, to the new and more scientifically based system which Rome had now adopted. But as often happens with the saints, the dream closest to the heart is realised only after their death, and so it was with Adomnán and Iona.

One of Adomnán's more notable diplomatic successes was occasioned by events in 684. It happened that Ecgfrith, king of Northumbria, raided the Irish kingdom of Brega, seat of the kings of Tara, and carried off many captives. Some time afterwards Ecgfrith was slain in battle and replaced by a new king, Aldfrith, who had been a pupil of Adomnán. The abbot went to him on a diplomatic mission and not only negotiated the release of sixty Irish captives but took them all back to Ireland.

To finish this short essay on 'the high sage of the western world', as one enthusiastic writer describes him, and as others would suggest, the founder of Scottish literature, we leave the last word to the *Annals of the Four Masters:* 'Adomnán, son of Ronan, abbot of Ia-Coluim Cille, died on 23 September, after having been twenty-six years in the abbacy, and after the seventy-seventh year of his age. Adomnán was a good man, according to the testimony of St Bede, for he was tearful, penitent, given to prayer, diligent, ascetic, and temperate; for he never used to eat except on Sundays and Thursdays only; he made a slave of himself to these virtues; and, moreover, he was wise and learned in the clear understanding of the holy scriptures of God.'

St Cainnech

Kenneth, or Kenny, is a very common name in Scotland. Not many Scots know it derives from an Irish saint, Cainnech. Other variations on his name are Canice and Kieran, common names in Kilkenny, the Irish city called after him.

Cainnech was a much-travelled man. We can trace his footsteps from his birthplace, in the Dungiven-Maghera area of Co Derry, over much of Ireland – Offaly, Westmeath, Tipperary, Dublin, Kilkenny – and Scotland – Kintyre, Glencoe, St Andrews, and the islands of Mull, Iona, Coll, Tiree, South Uist, Islay, Lismore – and as far as the Faroe Islands. Besides all that we are told that he was no stranger to Wales.

His early years
Cainnech's father, who was of the tribe of the Cianachta, is described in the Latin *Life* as a poet, a bard perhaps. The family are said to have been fairly poor and although the child had the honour of being baptised by Bishop Luirech – 'Luirech of the Poems' – at Maghera, his early years were spent in humble circumstances as a *buachaill bó* or cow-herd. He was born about the end of the second decade of the sixth century and on reaching maturity chose the religious life. Part of his training is said to have been done under St Cadoc of Wales at his monastery in Llancarvan, near the river Severn. Because his standard of obedience was so high, the bursar persecuted him; nevertheless, he persevered and was eventually ordained to the priesthood, and if the tradition be correct, made a pilgrimage to Rome. At some stage, too, he studied under St Finnian at Clonard and St Mobí in Glasnevin. In Glasnevin he enjoyed the companionship of Ciarán of Clonmacnoise and Colmcille.

The pilgrim in Scotland

The bond with Colmcille was strong. Adomnán, Colmcille's biographer, mentions Cainnech several times. On one occasion a great storm blew up when Cainnech was on his way to visit Iona, but Colmcille announced that he would arrive safely and to have a bath and refreshments ready for him and his companions. On another occasion Colmcille and some companions were caught in a storm at sea. In their distress they invoked St Cainnech, who was then in his monastery at Aghaboe in Ireland, and the storm abated. Again, five saints – Colmcille, Cainnech, Comgall, Brendan the Navigator, and Cormac O'Lehane the Sailor – were on the Island of Hinba [?Jura]. During Mass, celebrated by Colmcille, Brendan saw what Adomnán describes as a 'ball of fire like a comet burning very brightly on the head of Colmcille the whole time he stood before the altar offering the holy sacrifice and engaged in the most sacred mysteries'. Again, when Colmcille failed in his first mission to King Brude of the Picts, he was careful to take Cainnech and Comgall, two Irish Pictish speakers, with him on the second attempt. But Cainnech seems to have travelled further than Brude's stronghold at Inverness; he went as far as En-inis, the Island of Birds, in the Faroes.

When I was working in the Outer Hebrides I learned from a parish priest, Angus John McQueen, a delightful legend of Cainnech's days in a hermitage at Glencoe. I have already recounted this legend in my book, *A Pilgrim in Celtic Scotland*, but it is so beautiful and so typical of the Celtic world that it bears repeating here. The story goes that in the dark valley of Glencoe the saint had a little cell where the sun never shone. It was depressing to say the least. But the drawback was offset by a visit from the angel Gabriel every afternoon. On his arrival this particular day, the angel found the saint quite down in himself. 'What's the matter with you today?' said the angel. 'It's the mountains,' said Cainnech, 'They are so high about me and there isn't a shaft of sunshine ever to brighten my cell and it is hard to keep one's spirits up when one is experiencing that day in and day out.' The Angel Gabriel, always a bearer of good news, said, 'If that's your problem I can solve it at once and throw the mountain into the sea.' With that he got to work splitting that mountain with his angelic wings, but Cainnech stopped him, declaring that he was making a bad situation worse. And to this day the mountain exhibits a great fissure.

At the western end of Tiree there is a church of St Kenneth, *Kil-Chainnech*. As well as supporting Kenneth's community this Hebridean Island was the bread basket of Iona since it was not only fertile but enjoyed the longest hours of sunshine in all of Britain; hence the sobriquet, *Etica Terra*, 'land of wheat'. Other parts of Scotland associated with Kenneth include Kennoway in Fife, Laggan-Kenny by Loch Laggan in Invernessshire, together with a monastery of St Kenneth at Maiden Castle and another at St Andrews. The old name for St Andrews was Rigmond and there in the sixth century was a Kil-Rigmond, an Irish monastery under the rule of Cainnech. In that community lived another Irish monk named Riaghail, Latinised as *Regulus*, whose feast day is on 20 March. In post-medieval times there developed a fanciful legend to the effect that a fourth-century Greek monk named Regulus brought the relics of the apostle St Andrew to Scotland and deposited them at Rigmond which was ever after known as St Andrews. In reality, what happened was that in AD 736, during the tenure of the Irish abbot Tuathal, the Pictish king acquired the relics, deposited them at Rigmond and changed the name of the monastery to St Andrews.

Aghaboe and Kilkenny

Having lived and laboured in so many parts of Scotland, Cainnech returned to Ireland where he established a number of monasteries including one at Kilkenny West, Co Westmeath, where people still visit the holy well on 11 October. His principal foundation, however, was in an area largely coterminous with the present diocese of Ossory. Cainnech was welcomed to this ancient kingdom by one Colman whose father, Feradithe, was king. His arrival coincided with an *aonach* or fair where the king, riding a restive horse, was thrown and broke a femur. Cainnech made the sign of the cross over it and the man recovered. Feradithe subsequently granted Cainnech various tracts of land. One such, *Ach a' bó*, the cow field, became the site of his best known monastery, Aghaboe in Co Laois. Next Cainnech got permission to build a church beside the Nore, around which grew up the city of Kilkenny.

Cainnech's place of retreat was the island of Monahincha, in a now dried up lake a few kilometres from Roscrea, Co Tipperary. A curious legend describes how he one day saw a legion of demons flying overhead. One dropped down and Cainnech asked where they were all going. The demon replied that a man named Crom Dubh had died and they were going to collect him – they figured he was theirs because of his sins. Cainnech told the demon to call again on his way back and let him know how things went. On the return journey the same demon dropped in at Monahincha but he was limping. 'What happened you, my poor devil?' asked Cainnech. 'Well,' said the downcast demon, 'we thought Crom was ours, but St Patrick and a band of angels and saints came out and said that his generosity outweighed his sins, and with that they turned on us and drove us off with fiery arrows, one of which struck me in the leg and has left me maimed forever.'

Besides relating sympathetically with predatory demons, Cainnech was also skilled in human relations, as is evident from the story of the twelve Kerrymen who had designs on his life; somehow he won them over and they all became monks under his direction.

The *Lives* of Cainnech recount one story involving *Gíalcherd*, a savage custom learned perhaps from the Vikings (*gallcherd*, foreign art; or *gíalcherd*, treatment of hostages). It happened that Cainnech came upon a great crowd of people with their king. They were about to subject a little boy to this terribly cruel death. It involved tossing him onto a forest of upturned spears. Cainnech asked the king to liberate the boy but was refused. He then prayed to God and when the boy was tossed onto the spears the action neither killed nor harmed him except that for the rest of his days he remained cross-eyed as a result of looking in terror at the spear points. The king handed him over to Cainnech; and in the course of time Dolue Lebdeic (possibly meaning a person with a long-term disability) became a famous monk whose monastery is called *Kell Tolue*, Killaloe.

There is a tradition too that while he was resident in Monahincha Cainnech wrote the *Glas Cainic*, a sort of New Testament commentary. In Aghaboe he is said to have composed hymns and written a life of Colmcille. The *Lives* further inform us that Cainnech died at Aghaboe having received Viaticum from St Fintan of Clonenagh. His fame was so great that some chroniclers number him among the Twelve Apostles of Ireland.

The triumph of Kilkenny

After Cainnech's death about AD 600, the guardianship of his relics was disputed between Aghaboe and Kilkenny, a dispute which was resolved in favour of Kilkenny after some six centuries! The church of St Canneech, or Canice, in Kilkenny, begun in 1180 and finished by 1200, was not a cathedral but became so prior to 1250. At the Reformation in the sixteenth century it passed into the hands of the (Anglican) Church of Ireland. After the centuries of persecution the Catholics, finding themselves without their cathedral, laid the foundation stone of a new one on Sunday 18 August 1843. On its completion they dedicated it to Saints Mary and Kieran on 4 October 1857, the feast of Our Lady of the Rosary.

An unfailing light

For energy, zeal and impact, the life and personality of Cainnech must have equalled that of Colmcille himself, something all the more wondrous since his lower social status would not have given Cainnech the human advantages enjoyed by his illustrious contemporary. His residence in any given place cannot have been for very long, nor had he a biographer to chronicle it. And

yet, these sojourns are remembered even after fourteen centuries. One may well reflect on what it was in him that so im-
pressed itself on these communities that it still remains after
fourteen hundred years.

Guide to reading the chapters on St Columbanus and St Gall

St Columbanus

It is not surprising that people not overly familiar with early Irish saints tend to confuse two of the same name *Columba*, 'who had the greatest influence on the course of development of west-European civilisation in the middle ages.' Not only were they namesakes, they were also contemporaries. Using variations on the name, which means 'dove', the older man is usually known as Colmcille of Iona, the younger as Columban or Columbanus of Luxeuil and Bobbio.

Cleenish and Bangor

Columbanus was born in the 530s or early 540, probably on the Carlow-Wexford border. Knowledge of his early upbringing is skimpy but about the year 560 he became a student at the relatively new monastery of St Sinell on the island of Cleenish in Lough Erne. It was under Sinell, 'famous for his holiness and for his learning in sacred things', that our saint probably studied the sacred scriptures and ancillary subjects such as grammar, rhetoric and geometry. He returned home from Cleenish perhaps to discern more clearly where his future lay. Legend has it that he was strong, handsome, and much admired by the ladies, and turning his back on one of them in particular seems to have been a struggle of no small dimensions. On the other hand, we are told that when his mother threw herself across the threshold of the family home begging him not to leave, he stepped over her body and continued on his way without looking back. Before any twenty-first-century reader rises up in indignation on reading of this, it is important to add that the legend concerns the gospel injunction not to put one's hand to the plough and look back, rather than any insensitivity towards his mother. In reality, leaving home and breaking family ties was likely to have been the greatest pain of any young man or woman with their heart set on the monastic life.

After another stint in Cleenish, Columbanus decided to enter monastic life at St Comgall's foundation at Bangor in Co Down, a monastery destined to be one of the greatest of sixth-century Ireland. Comgall himself had been formed under the strict rule of St Fintan of Clonenagh in Laois, and although he has put his own stamp on Bangor, it continued to have much of the strictness of Fintan. The daily menu, for example, offered bread, vegetables and water, or if preferred, water, vegetables and bread! However, at a later date milk and milk products were permitted. It was in Bangor that Columbanus spent many years and there he was ordained to the priesthood and probably became head of the monastic school.

Ireland's First European

When he was about fifty years of age, probably in the year 590, Columbanus and twelve other Bangor monks sailed out of Belfast Lough bound for the continent of Europe. In the words of Cardinal Tomás Ó Fiaich, this man was in the fullest sense of the phrase, 'Ireland's first European,' a 'poet, scholar, abbot, preacher, saint, co-founder of western monasticism, associate of kings, correspondent of popes'. He was, says Ó Fiaich, the centre of controversy in his own day and has gone on to generate argument ever since.

We cannot say if the group had a more specific destination in mind than 'the continent.' They may have had a stopover in Cornwall (at St Colomb?). Living tradition has it that they first set foot on continental Europe about ten kilometres east of St Malo. A granite cross in the village of Cancale commemorates the event. If the rest of the continent were to commemorate the saint's stopping places by crosses there would be a veritable forest of them.

In 591, after a considerable amount of travelling, they found themselves in Burgundy. Here in the Vosges among the forested mountains they made their first permanent monastic settlement. This was Annegray, the site of an abandoned Roman fortification. Among the ruins was a temple of Diana which the Irishmen repaired and dedicated to that other founder of monasticism in western Europe, St Martin of Tours. Conditions at Annegray were such that the thought of the bread, vegetables and water enjoyed in Bangor smacked of high festivity. Jonas, the first biographer of the saint, says that their food was herbs, roots and the bark of trees! But the Lord heard their cry and kindly people both lay and clerical came to the aid of these devout settlers.

In the course of time so many came to Annegray that Columbanus sought a place of deeper seclusion where he could pray without interruption, especially on the vigils of Sundays and feast days. High upon a cliff there was a cave occupied by a bear but on being ordered by Columbanus the animal peremptorily vacated his residence and found himself a lair elsewhere. On another occasion, while at prayer, Columbanus found himself surrounded by twelve hungry wolves. The saint uttered the powerful prayer, 'O God come to my aid, O Lord make haste to help me' and with that the wolves decided on a different menu.

The life of Columbanus and his monks attracted local recruits in such numbers that soon another foundation was needed. The resourceful abbot found another old Roman fort, this time at Luxeuil about twelve kilometres distant, and yet again, when that community was proving too large, a third foundation was made five kilometres further north at Fontaine. The reputation of Luxeuil as a place of extraordinary learning, holiness and penitence soon outstripped the mother house. For the better ordering of these communities Columbanus wrote a monastic rule. Obedience was at its core, mortification, fasting, prayer and repentance the broad base, and the recitation of the Divine Office was held in such regard that it was no exaggeration for St Bernard of Clairvaux to write six centuries later: 'Into the foreign lands these swarms of saints poured as though a flood had risen.

Of these, one, St Columbanus, came to our Gallic lands and built
a monastery at Luxeuil, and was made there a great people. So
great a people was it, they say, that, choir following after choir,
the Divine Office went on unceasingly and not a moment of day
or night was empty of praise.' Twice a day the monks confessed
their sins both great and small and did appropriate penance
after private confession. It was this Irish practice that ultimately
revolutionised the church's discipline regarding the sacrament
of reconciliation.

Expulsion

Wolves and bears roamed the forests of Burgundy in those days,
but Columbnus and his monks were less troubled by them than
by wolves and bears of the human kind. Columbanus incurred
the wrath of the Queen Mother, Brunhilde, and her grandson because he denounced the sexual mores of the young king. He had
also ruffled the feathers of the Gaulish bishops not only by critic-
ising their lifestyle but also by not allowing them control over
his monasteries. The new approach to confession and his insist-
ence on monastic exemption were but two of many issues by
which Columbanus inaugurated a struggle between the Celtic
and Roman ecclesiastical systems that went on for well over a
century and 'in which the Synod of Whitby and the Bull of
Adrian IV were but episodes'.

Eventually, for Columbanus, the conflict led to his banish-
ment by Brunhilde and the king. In the year 610, when he was
nearing seventy years of age, Columbanus and his companions
set out under guard on a thousand kilometre treck to Nantes to
catch a ship for Ireland. Providence intervened. A three-day
storm blew the ship aground; the captain, realising that he was
dealing with more than ordinary natural forces, jettisoned the
cargo, refloated the ship, and set the monks back on continental
terra firma. A new chapter opened in the life of our saint.

'I am always moving from the day of my birth until the day
of my death,' he wrote. This was even more true of the remaining years of his life. His second crossing of the continent took

him to Soissons, Paris, Meaux, Metz, working spectacular miracles along the way. Next by boat down the Moselle to Koblenz, up the Rhine to Basle, on by Lake Zurich to Arbon in Switzerland, across Lake Constance (the Bodensee) to Bregenz in Austria, and finally over the Alps to Lombardy in northern Italy. It is at Milan in 614 that we find him preaching and in that same year he founded Bobbio in the foothills of the Appenines. Here he stayed until he gave forth his great soul to the Lord on 23 November of the following year.

Greatness

Columbanus was a writer of no mean ability and Latin style. Although much of his work is now lost, we still possess copies of his monastic Rules, Penitentials, letters, sermons and poetry. They reveal a man of rich personality, singleminded, austere, unworldly, courageous, firm in the freedom of the gospel, fearless in the face of civil or religious authority. He was typically Celtic in his combination of contradictory qualities, being by turns harsh and tender, humble and haughty, innovative and conservative. He respectfully reminded the Pope that Rome is important in the eyes of the Irish because it is St Peter's Chair: 'Though Rome be great and famous, she is great and renowned among us only because of that Chair.' And again, 'Power will rest with you just so long as your principles remain sound. The real key-bearer of the kingdom of heaven is he who opens up true knowledge to the worthy and shuts to the unworthy.' Urging the Pope to have courage he says that he must not allow 'the head of the church to be turned into its tail ... for among us [in Ireland] it is not who you are but how you make your case that counts.' While comfortable with diversity in detail, he was primarily concerned with the unity of the church. To the French bishops he wrote in 603, 'We are all members of one body, whether French, or British, or Irish or whatever our race.'

The influence of Columbanus on the continent can hardly be exaggerated, especially the wonderful impetus and direction he gave to the expansion of monasticism. 'He was,' says G. S. M.

Walker, 'a missionary through circumstances, a monk by voca-
tion; a contemplative, too frequently driven to action by the
world; a pilgrim, on the road to Paradise.' Perhaps the French
Foreign Minister, Robert Schuman, was right when he said, 'St
Columbanus is the patron saint of those who seek a united
Europe.'

St Gall

From the sixth to the ninth century, Irish monks swarmed onto the continent. Some were saints, some scholars, others both and more neither. Oftentimes having set out in search of solitude, they found themselves responding to the pastoral needs of their adopted lands, evangelising or re-evangelising a continent ravaged by lawless hoards of barbarians who had forced the frontiers of a declining Roman Empire. The 'dark ages' had descended where once high Roman civilisation was the wonder of the world. It was into this chaotic melting pot that Irish monks poured. Columbanus may not have been the first but he was certainly the most outstanding.

Of the twelve who left Bangor in his company, none is more famous than his close companion St Gall who outlived him by some ten years. Gall seems to have entered the monastic life at Bangor and remained there until his departure for the continent. For over twenty years he and Columbanus shared fortunes and misfortunes, only parting some three years before the death of Columbanus. From surviving records of their long relationship it would seem that Gall had a sort of 'middle management' role in the missionary expedition. He was also good at language and had a working knowledge of at least one of the Germanic dialects which allowed for communication with the local people and their rulers. In fact there still exists in the great library of St Gallen in Switzerland a Latin-German 'dictionary' in Irish script thought to have been composed by St Gall.

Murder plots
After the attempted expulsion, when Columbanus, Gall and the

others had been put on board ship at Nantes and blown back to land again, they travelled north east and journeyed up the Rhine, for which occasion Columbanus wrote his *Rowing Song* to create a rhythm for the oarsmen and derive maximum value from the energy they expended in going against the strong current of that great river. From the Rhine they passed on to the river Aare, to the Limmat and thence to the shores of Lake Zurich. Here a pagan German tribe still worshipped the god Woden. Gall was incensed at such behaviour and not only preached against it but took direct action by setting fire to their temple and throwing their sacrificial material into the lake. On learning of a plot to murder Gall, the Irish group moved on swiftly to Arbon on the southern shore of Lake Constance where they were befriended by Fr Willimar, the local priest in that old Roman town.

It was from Fr Willimar that the wandering group learned of yet another deserted Roman fort, this one about twenty five kilometres across the lake at Bregenz in the Austrian Tyrol, described as a place of 'surpassing fertility and romantic grandeur'. On arrival they found there a little church once dedicated to St Aurelia but now used as a pagan temple serving the needs of the latest Germanic tribes to settle there. As happened by Lake Zurich, it fell to Gall to do most of the preaching among the locals since he 'had no small knowledge of the barbaric speech.' Once again taking a direct approach with the pagans, he told them to turn away from worshipping the bronze images with which they had decorated the little church, and with that he proceeded to strip the walls, smash the images, and consign the lot to the depths of Lake Constance, the Bodensee. Assassination and reprisal was uppermost in the minds of many but there were others who came to follow the way of Jesus. Columbanus rededicated the church, sprinkled the building with holy water, signed the altar with holy oil, put relics of the saints in it, covered it with a white cloth and celebrated Mass. The monks went in procession to the event while Gall and a deacon chanted appropriate psalms. A superficial peace prevailed.

Gall was assigned to the making and mending of nets because he was a good fisherman. So successful was he on the Bodensee that he not only met the needs of the community but had stocks for sharing with visitors and strangers. Nevertheless, the pagans hadn't forgotten what had been done to their idols. They succeeded in getting the local duke, Gunzo, to proclaim expulsion of the monks on the pretext of interference with fishing and gaming rights. Then two of the brethren, who had gone in search of a missing cow, were assassinated: moving on became urgent. Their stay in Bregenz had been little more than a year, and though many of the monks had fallen in love with the beautiful spot, further stay was unthinkable.

A painful obedience

It was at this point that the two friends Gall and Columbanus not only parted from Bregenz but parted from one another as well. The circumstances surrounding the break-up are not wholly clear. Gall was ill with a fever and felt unable to travel. Columbanus was not convinced that the illness was that serious. Walafrid Strabo, a ninth-century biographer of Gall, describes the parting as follows: 'When the time for their departure was at hand, Gall fell suddenly ill of a fever. He threw himself at the abbot's feet and said he was suffering from a severe illness and was unable for the journey. Columbanus said to him: "Brother, I know that now it seems a heavy burden to you to suffer further fatigue for my sake. Nevertheless, this I enjoin on you before I go, that so long as I live in the body, you do not dare to celebrate Mass".' The decision seems harsh but without knowledge of the full circumstances, who can judge?

Columbanus set his face towards the Alps and Italy. Gall returned to Fr Willimar at Arbon. There he slowly recovered his health, assisted by Willimar and two deacons, Magnoald and Theodore, whom Willimar had assigned to be Gall's helpers. Another deacon, Hiltbold, helped him find a suitable hermitage in the locality. The land was fertile, there was a spring of water. The woods and rocks afforded shelter to wild beasts – bears, boars, reptiles and ravenous wolves. Here he built a little church in honour of the Blessed Virgin Mary. The story goes that while he was at prayer a bear came out of the woods, but Gall threw him a loaf of bred and sent him on his way.

When Gaudentius, the Bishop of Constance, died in about 614, a three day assembly of clergy of all levels, together with the influential laity, unanimously chose Gall to be their new bishop. The chief promoter of this choice was none other than Gunzo, his erstwhile enemy, whose daughter, Frideburga, Gall had recently healed. The saint turned down the request on the grounds that he had been forbidden to celebrate Mass by his abbot Columbanus, and furthermore that church law required a candidate, except in exceptional circumstances, to be a native of the country. On being further requested to name another suitable candidate St Gall suggested the deacon John, an outstanding disciple of his and native of the area. Tradition has it that on the occasion of the installation of the new bishop Gall preached the sermon in Latin but for the sake of those who did not understand that language Bishop John translated it into the vernacular.

Reconciliation

Meanwhile across the Alps in Bobbio, Columbanus was nearing his end. The old warrior for Christ hadn't forgotten the days of his prime and the decades spent side by side with Gall as they faced the unknown, the dangers, the hardships, the set-backs and the joys of winning new peoples to their Lord. Nor had he forgotten his last injunction, perhaps spoken in haste with that haughtiness of which he was capable. Now at the end he had one last request for his attendant: when I am dead send my staff to Gall. But before that staff was delivered, Gall had a premonition of events. Calling his deacon Magnoald, he told him to prepare everything necessary for the celebration of Mass because 'I have learnt in a vision that my Lord and father Columbanus has passed from the miseries of this life to the joys of paradise this day. Therefore I must offer Mass for his repose.'

On the death of the abbot of Luxeuil in 627, Gall was approached by half a dozen monks from that monastery with a request to become the new abbot but again he turned down the request, this time pleading age and his general inadequacy. Keeping up the tradition of his native land Gall gave the Luxeuil delegation a *céad míle fáilte* and entertained them as generously as his monastery and power of fishing and miracle-working would allow, before sending them on their way with a letter refusing the high honour offered him. The truth is that Gall was essentially a hermit but out of apostolic zeal chose to continue to the end of his life preaching and instructing, chiefly among the most abandoned souls in the mountainous parts of the country.

It was probably on the feast of St Remigius on 1 October 630 that Gall and Fr Willimar, together with a crowd of people, had a final meeting and a prayerful liturgy. Shortly after that he fell ill with a fever and died in the arms of Willimar on 16 October. He was the last of that gallant and saintly band who forty years previously had sailed out of Belfast Lough having committed themselves irrevocably to becoming pilgrims for Christ's sake.

Postscript

With the passage of time there grew up around St Gall's hermitage first a monastery, then a city, a diocese, and finally the Canton of St Gallen. The monastic library there is world famous particularly for its collection of mediaeval Irish manuscripts; and the monastic church, rebuilt in rococo style in the mid-eighteenth century and now serving as the cathedral, is a sight to behold. Some years ago when on pilgrimage (monks never go on holidays, they always go on pilgrimage!) I visited Bregenz and St Gallen and celebrated Mass at Gall's tomb in the cathedral crypt. To share the joy of that occasion I sent a postcard to a dear and saintly Irish confrère named Gall, who lived in our monastery at Esker, Athenry, and who had been a missionary in the Philippine Islands during the 1930s and 40s. The reception of that card together with the knowledge that I had celebrated the Holy Eucharist for his welfare at the tomb of his patron was never forgotten by him and cemented our bond more deeply. Now that he too has returned to the Lord of Glory, I have to make a distinction in my prayer – St Gall of Switzerland, and St Gall of Esker.

Other books by the same author
published by Columba Press

Irish Catholic Spirituality
1856072436 160 pages £8.99

The Music of What Happens
Celtic Spirituality – A View from the Inside
185607174X 128pp £6.99

A Pilgrim in Celtic Scotland
1856071936 128pp £6.99